Praise

'Being truly independent is a goal many people have for themselves. It implies being financially free from a job, ambivalent to economic swings and unafraid of life's twists and turns. It's a mindset as much as a financial benchmark. In this book, Andrew shares his experience and wisdom from many years working with people to achieve this level of independence and his own experiences. Making the right decisions as early as possible is incredibly important. He shares the tactical ideas and the broader mindset required to stay on the path towards the day that you are truly independent.'

— **Daniel Priestley**, entrepreneur and author
    of *How to Raise Entrepreneurial Kids*

'This book has reinforced my knowledge and outlook while providing me with new information and unique viewpoints. Resonate is an excellent word to describe my personal attitude towards this book and its content. The message is well constructed and is fluent. Further, it feels to be conveyed with more sincerity than other books that I have read, and not exaggerated or sounding salesman-like. It realistically portrays how attainable wealth creation truly is, as it is broken down and elaborated on thoroughly.'

— **Connor Turner**, apprentice compliance
    officer, Truly Independent Ltd

'A very inspiring read – every young person should read this and incorporate the lessons taught in this book into their lives from as early on as possible. Andrew talks about the power of asset accumulation and passive income in a jargon-free way using examples which we can all relate to, helping to further educate the younger generation about money and the importance of managing it correctly from day one. I would highly recommend this book to all who wish to leave the working trap and reach financial independence.'

— **Ewa Breska**, mortgage adviser and influencer

Work to Wealth

Work because you
want to and do more
with your income

Andrew Goodwin

Rethink

For school sixth-formers, college students, apprentices, undergraduates, postgraduates and all young adults trying to find their way.

For anyone who wants a better life for themselves and is willing to change.

For everyone, out of work, in work, who has to work or who wants to work.

Contents

Foreword   **1**

Preface   **5**

Introduction   **9**

The problem   11

The solution   12

Who should read this book?   14

Why I'm writing this book   15

PART ONE   Work   **17**

Work because you want to, not
because you have to   19

1   The Route To Wealth Starts With Work   **21**

Sheer hope   22

Social media – the teenager trap   26

Move to improve   27

Settled and happy in your job   28

Earned Disposable Income – EDI   31

The hourly rate time trap   35

Don't work because you have to   38

Key points   39

2 **Political Promises**   **43**

The political trap   44

The pension trap   45

Stop spending, start saving and investing   51

Debt – a very common problem   55

Key points   56

3 **Active And Passive Income**   **59**

Big field   60

Wealth is available to everyone,
not just the fortunate   63

Income follows assets (follow income)   65

Assetise your income   68

Asset delegation   72

Key points   74

4 **Asset Accumulation**   **77**

When you work, your income should
be working too   77

Types of assets   79

Double your saving principle   82

Asset partners   89

Key points   91

5 Meaningful Change   95

Change requires desire, courage and
perseverance   96

COVID-19 – forced change   97

Resolutions without fear   98

Life of credit – an opportunity cost   104

Make more money – become indispensable   108

Key points   111

PART TWO   Wealth   113

Do more with your income than
spend, spend, spend   114

6 Millionaire Measures   117

Get rich quick   118

Millionaire test   120

Cashflow   131

If I am an asset, do I have a value?   134

Key points   135

7 Powerful Investment   137

Saving is not investing   139

Investing requires expert advice   145

Key points   155

8   Beautiful Property   157

Your home is not an
income-producing asset, yet!   159

Property as a business   162

Key points   172

9   Aspiring Business Owners   175

In a job or in business   177

Business start-up   179

On it, not in it   184

Business for sale   188

Mergers and acquisitions   193

Key points   193

10   Independent Financial Advice   197

Not all financial advisers are the same   198

Everyone should have an IFA   200

Aims, goals and ambitions   210

Key points   212

Final Thoughts   215

Your Call To Action   **217**

    Investing – how do I get started?   218

Notes   **219**

Acknowledgements   **227**

The Author   **229**

Foreword

In this important book Andrew conveys some key aspects to living life to the full, typifying his own approach to life.

Social mobility is defined as being 'better off than your parents', but many people these days simply aren't, even though the UK is the fifth or sixth richest, and arguably the best, place to live in the world. Social mobility is the key to mankind's progress and happiness, yet for the last few years has gone into reverse. There is a disjoint between our youngsters, and their ability to thrive in the world of work.

On a day-to-day basis my organisations deal primarily with trying to bring about social mobility. Businesses are the key to this, not just educational establishments.

We do not have quotas to include (and therefore exclude) certain types of people; we are truly inclusive and intentionally blind to lots of items mentioned by elitists as necessary. By following inclusive guidelines, we also have one of the most diverse businesses in the UK.

The Social Mobility Pledge signed by nearly 1,000 major businesses and education organisations specifies three broad requirements: name-blind contextual recruitment, so that you don't exclude based on biases or external quotas; in-house apprenticeships and placements; and a link to a school or schools so pupils can see what the world of work is really like.[1] This creates a pathway between education and work. What is necessary is giving people a chance, even a second or third chance, recruiting the best you can based on attitude and then ability (not a common or garden degree on a vague subject), and continuing to offer training for the rest of their employment, constantly. And have fun and make money.

Education is of course important but, without the ability to get into work, is largely wasted. We have become distracted and have forgotten that without a job, there is no money, there is only debt; and to become wealthy you need to control debt and put it in its right place – a means to gain long-term assets, not a means to pay for a holiday – early. To do any of that you need to get a job.

I was lucky (and still am): when I grew up there were lots of jobs. None were sold as being glamorous, but all of them, as now, prepare you for life by mixing you with working adults, who will hopefully keep you right. The rest is up to you. When you get paid, you stand up straight and your hand goes out to pay, to give, not to just receive.

So, I would urge you to immediately buck the trend; be bold, don't follow the rest, get making money and use your imagination in becoming wealthy. It is a strange thing when people say money doesn't bring you happiness. Only those with money could say that, so how would the rest know? Of course, money won't buy you happiness, but living without money certainly doesn't bring anything but misery.

As Goethe allegedly once said: 'Whatever you can do, or dream you can, begin it/Boldness has genius, power and magic within it.'[2]

Read this book, follow it, be bold.

David Harrison
founder of the Harrison Foundation

Preface

'Opportunity is missed by most people because it is dressed in overalls and looks like work.'
— Thomas Edison[3]

If you compare yourself to those ostensibly wealthier than you, you may never truly achieve. If you compare yourself to those ostensibly poorer than you, you may never truly progress. Comparison will keep you within these boundaries, in walled frustration.

We live in a society where everything and everyone is compared. We are politically, economically and morally urged in the direction of fairness for all. We are encouraged to be impartial and to behave without favouritism or discrimination. Everything we do must be seen to be for the benefit of others and not just ourselves.

I understand this thinking that includes everyone and benefits all equally, but there is a problem. While such socialist ideals appear logical and fair, in reality they don't actually succeed. Socialism will always malfunction when following an equalising strategy rather than encouraging individuals to succeed in their own right. Trying to equalise is the Robin Hood, fast-track route to achieving only temporary adjustment, driven by observations of unfairness and inequality: temporary because it is fragile by design and only succeeds to patch society's problems merely as appeasement for the poor.

Successful people breed success and the most successful almost always give back, either directly through philanthropic engagement or indirectly through job creation. Socialism follows capitalism and not the other way around. A more equal and fair society can only be built following the drive and ambition of others who are encouraged to search for more, create more and improve more. They generate the wealth that socialism relies upon.

That said, capitalism can falter too, especially when the successful neglect the people that helped them achieve in the first place. I am a firm believer in capitalism, but I recognise that its far reaches can leave others behind and stretch financial fairness to the elastic limits of excess and greed.

I would describe myself as a 'caring, compassionate capitalist'. I want to guide young people away from fast routes to adulthood and their struggle to be seen or heard in the distorted expectations of the social media society. Young people have lost the necessary, steady bridges to maturity and appear to have lost their sense of real life itself.

It is important to encourage individuals to be successful and release their entrepreneurial flair while inculcating a culture of responsibility and the importance of working partnerships and individual cooperation on the journey. We actually need each other and when we recognise leaders, then we must support them. As leaders we equally must recognise the workers and support them too.

We are all together but there must be space for individuals to pursue their own dreams: to define wealth by their own definitions and satisfy their own desires, protected from opinion and negativity. We all have to work for someone, so work because you want to and not because you have to. Make work the provider of your wealth.

If young individuals want to be wealthy enough not to rely on having to work for a living, then the way they think about work and money has to change. In particular, what they do with their working income has to change.

The success of this shift simplifies down to a deliberate change in mindset, from the false world of social media back into the real world of work.

Introduction

Imagine that the seat you sit on at work might one day have an envelope taped to the underside, in which will be a cheque payable to you for £1,000,000. If this were true you would check the underside of that seat every day.

You would not miss a day at work, just to make sure you could check the underside of that seat. As each day passed, you might feel there was more chance of the envelope being there tomorrow, than today. Eventually, if you had not found it yet and equally had not missed a day at work, you would find the envelope on your last day at work before retiring; what a day!

In reality, this is not imagination. People work all their lives until they have accumulated enough (often in a pension pot) to retire. What they don't realise is that the money has been there all the time, they just do not yet know it or appreciate it. The median take-home pay in the UK adds up to over £1.2 million over a forty-year working life.[4] So it is there but it is drip-fed to you in small chunks and disguised by false ideas of how work is portrayed and wrapped in your misunderstanding of money.

Underpinned by the story of my personal journey from work to wealth, the contents of this book will change the way you think about money and what going to work is really about. Armed with this information you will be on your way to being that wealthy person you would rather be.

The title of this book, *Work to Wealth*, is my attempt to join two stereotypical classes to an evident and achievable connection. A person's wealth comes from a background of work; but few who work become wealthy, because they don't know how.

My underlying message is to forget political promises, the inaccurate tales on social media, lessons delivered by your parents, the lure of lucky windfalls, the mystique and the jargon about money and to simplify it all into one single function: take control of your own destiny and set about accumulating your own wealth and social mobility. By far the most confident and best route to wealth is to work so you can collect money; like a collector of stamps or beer mats, your job is to collect money and to invest it wisely.

Throughout the book I will explain the barriers to wealth that begin at home, develop at school and grow through adult life. These barriers are invisible and knowing them, expecting them, means you can overcome them. Everyone wants to be wealthy, but they also want it quickly and when wealth does not arrive, they give up. Their dreams turn to hope, hope turns to disappointment, disappointment turns to regret, regret turns to surrender and surrender manifests in blame. When you hear someone placing blame, they have given up!

The problem

Young people are first exposed to their parents' approach to finances. School's ideas soon follow, and maybe further education enhances opinion a little more. Then the exposure to social media messages takes over. Most media financial messages are predictable: based on an individual's economic security and sketched from a government's political strategy. These financial lessons change little from the old economics principles of 'a good education leads to a good job'. If you get an excellent job with a good income, our educators tell us that you will be secure for life. Your bank will provide a mortgage to fund your first real investment, a home. Finally, after years of working where you may have experienced and enjoyed the spoils of promotion, you will retire on a solid pension. And be thankful for it! In between, you continue to work, earn, raise a family and accept the weekends and holidays as your reward time, for play.

People do not understand that working for an income is trading time for money, and this message is still not getting through. They continue to work for a living because they have to.

Over 32 million people are working in the UK today.[5] The actual odds of these 32 million individuals becoming rich, wealthy or millionaires depend on many things such as age, education, race and background. However, Wikipedia reports that only 8.4% of the adult population in North America are millionaires.[6] In comparison, less than 2.7% are millionaires in Europe, including the UK. Behind these figures is the sad fact that, of the 32 million current workers in the UK alone, 31.1 million may never be wealthy, because they just don't know how or what to do to improve their chances.

The solution

Put simply, do more with your income. Invest it and go back to work to get some more. Work is where the money is. Working for money to invest is a reason to work, a habit, or perhaps a good kind of addiction.

This book aims to help and persuade the reader that accumulating assets is the key to wealth. Working for a living is exchanging time for money. When time runs out, so does the ability to earn money. Working people must stop spending their hard-earned income and start investing to accumulate assets. The assets you accumulate, in turn, need to produce income. Investing your hard-working income should begin as early as possible; accumulating assets takes time and management. Be prepared to give something up, to make space for a better way of living.

It is passive income that determines your wealthiness, and not capital. A million units of money do not necessarily provide a high (or even any) revenue. I will introduce and focus on four main asset groups: investments, property, and business – each of which produce a passive income. The fourth asset group is you. If managed well, these four assets can all work to bring you wealth, essentially, all at the same time.

Committing to change, taking financial advice, appointing mentors and professional managers are sure ways of transferring your work into wealth. You can achieve wealth from the meekest of financial standings.

Who should read this book?

While this book is for everyone, I'd like young people to read it because they often have a skewed perception of work and earnings, particularly school sixth-formers and college students since the earlier they learn about money, the better advantage they can take of the opportunities available to them.

Only the top 1% of all adults earn more than £120,000 per annum.[7] Young people believe it is more like 10%. They can be further surprised to learn that the remaining 99% earn an average of around £30,000.[8] This perception is distorted by possessions and perceived lifestyles. When young people see images of someone driving an expensive car or standing next to a five-bedroom house or sunbathing on a luxury yacht, they don't see that the earnings required to sustain this lifestyle are above £250,000 per year. In fact. only the top 0.5% receive this level of income.[9]

We are taught to gain qualifications that will lead us to employment. In turn, this employment will provide an enjoyable life followed by a satisfying retirement, we hope: the higher the qualification, the better the career and the earlier we may be able to afford to retire. While this principle may be true, we are taught nothing about money, mortgages or alternative ways of living. This book is aimed at everyone since everyone can save, invest and accumulate assets. Everyone can have an independent financial adviser too and everyone should do.

Why I'm writing this book

Drawing on my time working in the financial industry, years of study and culminating in having built a multi-million-pound business, I aim to share my knowledge with the reader.

I have an honours degree in Actuarial Mathematics and Statistics and have worked in financial services for more than twenty-five years, gaining valuable experience on how financial advice is distributed across the UK. I have seen changing business models and changing technology and survived downturns when many others have failed.

The knowledge and experience I have gained have allowed me to write an Amazon #1 bestseller, *The Happy Financial Adviser*.[10] In 2010 I set up my own firm called Truly Independent Ltd, providing independent financial advice across the UK, which now has UK-wide distribution and is well known in the industry. Separately, the actions I have taken with my personal income have made me wealthy, not just the actions taken to grow the company.

If you know how working can help you to achieve your dreams, even from the lowest of beginnings, you will view work differently because that is where your wealth starts.

This book will teach the reader how to achieve wealth by explaining the issues we face every day and providing a route to solve these problems. Those who follow this route with hard work, effort and energy will achieve their dreams.

I have assetised my income; why don't you?

PART ONE

WORK

It is generally accepted that you have to work for a living unless you are one of the fortunate, wealthy few.

Unless you are born into wealth, inherit wealth or have a significant win on the lottery, the only means to accumulate wealth is through your ability to work. Part One of this book is all about refining your reason for working. You need to sharpen your skills for more substantial results and a better working experience. Working alone won't make you wealthy; also, and quite separately, you must work at becoming wealthy.

To achieve wealth, you first need to spend time understanding what work should really be about. This book's title (*Work to Wealth*) is a reminder that you go to work because you want to be wealthy and not just because you have to work to pay the bills. This is the mindset needed for anyone who wants to be wealthy (or wealthier than you are). If you are working and nowhere near being wealthy, the title reminds you to do something different. You need to start to make changes to your working habits, knowledge, skills and influence. And to make changes in the way you treat the income that you generate from your hard work.

Work is both a noun and a verb. It is a place of work and an activity at work. I recall a message I heard many years ago: 'If you're going to work, go to work; otherwise, don't go'. I work all the time, though rarely at work. I think, breathe and plan work and am never out of work, always thinking about work. When I am at work, I am usually putting my work into action, working.

Part One will consider the true value of work relative to income and show how these words come together to forge a new way of thinking about money for a better financial outcome. Finally, I will introduce you to income-producing assets (in Chapter 4) and to 'assetising' your income (in Chapter 3 and extensively after that).

You will need to open your mind to all financial opportunities and be prepared to change. But the good news is, there is no big secret to wealth, though commitment is necessary. In this book I describe moments when I experienced an epiphany and those who (like me) have grasped these moments and used them, have changed their lives.

Work because you want to, not because you have to

Stripping everything back to the basic principles, I first want to give you a gift: a better reason to work. By creating simple and achievable financial goals, you will leap out of bed in the morning eager to earn. Those who hate work need alternative reasons to work and to know what they should be doing with their hard-earned income.

Those who enjoy working and being at work may have somewhere lost the drive to move out of this comfort zone. You need to use the fact you like work as a springboard to a better working experience, one that edges you closer to wealth.

Do more with your income

Those who spend their savings will eventually run out of money, unless those savings are significant. Income is what you want, not capital. Investopedia defines income as 'money that a person or a business receives in return for working, providing a product or service, or investing capital'.[11]

We all need a basic income to survive. Without pay we will achieve little and struggle to buy living essentials. Income is vital. It's what you do with it that matters and the wealthy know this; by studying this book, so will you.

You can earn income from working or receive income from assets. Investopedia describe an 'asset' as 'a resource with economic value that an individual, corporation or country owns or controls with the expectation that it will provide a future benefit'. It says 'an asset can be thought of as something that, in the future, can generate cash flow'.[12]

Understand assets and you are on your way to your first epiphany moment.

Mobilise your way to wealth

The purpose of this Part of the book is to focus on the idea of working to acquire assets and not because you have to. These assets can provide you with a passive income so you don't have to keep working. As well as assets and how to monetise them, I will also discuss the power of savings and introduce the double your saving principle – simply, doubling something results in something bigger, so if you want twice the omelette, you need twice the eggs.

This will mean changing your mindset away from working just to earn income to live on. You will need to change how you view your income and be prepared to do more with it. The terminology I use will become natural to you by the end of this book, to the point, I hope, where you can articulate these ideas to your friends and family.

1
The Route To Wealth Starts With Work

With some research on the internet it doesn't take long to discover there is a savings crisis in the UK. In 2014 HSBC reported that 44% of the population had less than £2,000 in savings.[13] By 2016 The Money Advice Service said this had dropped to £100.[14] The same searches today find similar results. Nearly half of the population has 'at best' no more than a single month's income in savings. This is all down to the way we live and treat work. Changing this outcome is less of a challenge than you might first think.

If an individual has little or no savings, then what should they do to improve their situation?

First, they need a reason to change followed by an achievable target and the commitment to achieving that target. If you want to make a difference to your life and achieve your dreams, then there has to be a shift in how you think about work and income.

The dreams I hear people talk about are primarily modest and therefore reasonably achievable. They include:

- To own your home outright without a mortgage

- To drive a luxury car

- To run your own business

- To work in a job you love

- To travel the world

- To simply do nothing at all

There are plenty of similar examples and thoughts from the population dreaming of a better way to live. These people are frustrated with the daily churn and feel trapped in their work, a way of life not of their choosing. The answer is actually in work but let us start by looking at mindsets to avoid.

Sheer hope

Truthfully, almost everyone who struggles dreams of being financially free to choose an alternative lifestyle. It is the reason why the UK National Lottery does so well. Lottoland.co.uk report on their website that 'a staggering 70% of the UK's over-18s take part in the national lottery on a regular basis, which is close to 45 million people'.[15] It states that at least 50% of the population play the lottery once a month, on average buying a minimum of three tickets each week.

Considering the facts, it could be argued that the 44% of the population who have less than £2,000 are among the same 50% who buy three lottery tickets each week. Although the lottery is just a bit of fun for some, for many a lottery win is their hoped-for saviour. They feel the potential million-pound win is worth the small sacrifice of their time and money, despite the chances of winning being a staggering 14 million to 1. It's not much different in America either, with 57%, nearly 181 million people, buying at least one lottery ticket each year. Their hope of achieving their dreams through the lottery is nothing short of delusional and a terrible plan. What is impressive is their diligence in making regular time to buy that lottery ticket, addictively if you like; as if the week they do not buy one will be the week they would have won. Having started, they cannot now stop. Stopping would be sacrilege. If only they could redirect that same lottery time and diligence towards a more likely return on their time and outlay: something that provides a much better payoff, something more dependable than sheer hope.

Scratch-cards are equally overbought. Around 25% of Brits buy a scratch-card every month. What is astonishing is that 55–65-year-olds are more likely to buy a scratch-card than any other age group. Is it because they have more money to spend on a bit of fun or because they feel it's their last hope at that age? I will let you ponder that conundrum; however, if you are over 65 and retired, you are the least likely to buy a lottery ticket!

The problem develops further in the children. The allure of *things* is strong, so they spend money rather than saving it. This issue is not helped by the fact that there is less and less 'cash' in the system, and seemingly no desire for it. Fewer people carry cash than ever before but they have a seemingly endless supply with a touch of plastic. Bleep! Bleep! And the item is bought.

How can we teach our children the actual value of money once it is all virtual? The answer is to teach children about future value and self-responsibility. Every adult knows they need money of some kind to live, and that this is primarily earned through work. The knowledge behind this thinking is limited. Why not avoid sheer hope and use your working time to your advantage, building a life you really want and desire rather than trying to win it?

The minimum age to buy a lottery ticket in the UK has risen from 16 to 18 years old. The authorities finally realise how early indulgence in chance sends a damaging message to our youth. We should be more positive about the wonderful experiences and benefits and certainties of a working life, rather than the lottery life of sheer hope.

Starting work in hope

When you arrive at working age, say 16, and start the next phase of your life with a basic education and no money or skills, you can feel totally lost, forgotten and destitute. You could also feel this way after you have completed higher education. At age 21, even with your degree certificate in your hand, you will struggle to get that first job. I have felt this struggle.

Sadly, nearly one-third of the UK working population say they do not enjoy their jobs.[16] You might not work if you didn't need the money but you do need it, so you work, perhaps reluctantly. Annoyingly, there is no other choice. None of the 'get rich quick' ideas have paid off. The horse you were told about fell at the last fence; the pyramid scheme never got off the ground for you; the lottery has failed you too, delivering nothing but a £10 note. There is no inheritance due, certainly not just yet, and there is no sign of any sudden windfall. You only have you, and you have no choice but to work.

You have the desire to improve your circumstances, progress and move up the social ladder. What you need is a job. A good job. With prospects. This job will solve your problems and provide you with the freedom you deserve. If you have debts (a student loan, perhaps), you need to sort them out. Your future depends on that job. Right?

Social media – the teenager trap

This is a relatively new phenomenon. Teenagers and young adults spend so much time on social media platforms that it is challenging for them to see the truth. Most can decipher the chiff from the chaff, but some cannot. For many, their looks are more influenced by social media than other media or traditional advertising. Products are promoted to follow the current body image trends: a particular body-shape, say. Product providers use freely available data to catch the trends affecting behaviour. Some would say promotion shades into propaganda.

Celebrities start this interest. Their open availability to everyone who has a smartphone is significant and the way they use social media is a powerful influence on teenage decisions. Teenagers are easily attracted to celebrity lifestyles, commodities or behaviour that they exhibit on social media. Some celebrities are paid to promote products and ideas and while many foster good behaviour and values, unfortunately, the good merges with the bad.

To be responsible people, teenagers need consistent and accurate information but we may see a young person emerge from their teenage years to a world where work and the importance of work is strange to them. Moreover, working to contribute to their own and the broader social construct is equally unusual. They have seen celebrities and superstars in huge houses, driving expensive sports cars, and wearing the latest fashion and accessories. They can be desperate to follow this lifestyle, unable to understand the value of money and borrowing irresponsibly to access money to spend on the products they see on their screens.

Sadly, unless we educate young minds in school, it will take them many years as adults to realise the mistakes they make with credit. There is a strong need for financial education and the truth about work before they enter it.

Move to improve

If you live in a large city, you will have plenty of jobs to search for but greater competition. In the country there will be fewer job vacancies but also fewer candidates seeking those jobs. You will typically earn more in the city than the country, but living costs are higher there.

One failing of many workers today is lack of willingness to move: to leave town and seek their fortune elsewhere. Many attend university and return to their hometown for work. Why? A lack of flexibility limits your opportunity. You have to be prepared to move to improve your situation.

Suppose you have reached the age of 30, say, and never moved away to work. In that case, knowledge about work and money is restricted to the people and experiences around you, your family, friends and acquaintances. If you only buy red socks, you can wear red socks or no socks. You think your mind is full of knowledge, but that knowledge is restricted to the world immediately around you. Your sock drawer might be stuffed, but only with red socks.

Settled and happy in your job

In a recent YouGov survey of 1,133 British workers, 'two-thirds of Brits say they are in jobs they like or love, while only half consider themselves as well paid'.[17] More than one in seven stated they dislike or hate their jobs and nearly a quarter thought they were poorly paid. That is sad.

Further, YouGov asked the question 'Would you rather have a job you hate that pays well, or a job you love that pays poorly?' To this, 64% said they would rather have a poorly paid job they loved and only 18% would take a well-paid job they hated. There appears to be an accepted trade-off between misery and money. Could the accepted challenge be to find work you like that pays well?

The survey cross-referred the Brits in reasonably well- or very well-paid jobs, and those who either like or love their job, revealing that almost a third are in both groups. That means more than two-thirds could do better. These people might already be thinking life could be better. This book will help them seek more pay or a job they prefer with the same pay, but it is the settled and happy that I also want to wake up. If you are in the third that both like or love your job and feel fairly or well paid, then you are already heading down the road of opportunities lost.

EXAMPLE: THE WORKING TRAP

Before you have a penny to your name, if you have secured employment then you have access to credit. For a young adult in employment the lure of a shiny new car and the freedom it offers is too appealing. Before long, the employed income turns to debt.

Of course, you don't see this coming. You are enjoying life. Especially now that you have the job you like or love and are happy with your pay. Your job is no longer the problem. Enjoying that income becomes the next barrier. Spending is your reward for your achievements and the pleasures take over.

Now there is an added reason to work – not just to earn enough to live on, but enough to feed the new lifestyle debts. Life continues. The weekends become the only time to play and the desire to enjoy oneself after a busy week working leads to spending more money.

On Monday, it's back to work; that is, if you work office hours, of course. The need for money is fuelled when a partner arrives whom you shower with gifts. Then the lure of a house comes into the foreground, either rental or maybe to own a property with, of course, a mortgage. Soon, married or not, there is a baby on the way and the start of a permanent debt to which only love is returned.

The working trap is slowly but surely engulfing this individual. The only sure way out is to work longer hours and increase the income. This involves more time at work which needs more significant rewards, so the more expensive holiday abroad comes into the picture.

The working trap is soon triggered; there is no obvious way out. This person is now working because they have to and not because they are inspired. They may like the work they do or loathe it; at this point it makes no difference. This is the point where they realise it's not money they desire, or dream about, it is freedom – having more time. More time to spend with their partner. More time to spend playing with their children. More time to complete those DIY jobs they have started and not yet finished. In fact, it's more time for the simple things in life that can cost little. Love, companionship and a desire to breathe for a minute. Something they try to find on holiday. The working trap is firmly triggered when the annual holiday becomes the surrogate to dream about.

This person may not be you, or at least you don't think it's you. Test yourself, then. Think of your family, friends and colleagues for a moment and see whether you can name someone in this situation. Do you see that person?

Earned Disposable Income – EDI

There is no doubt that the key to any future success is to first escape the working trap. There are two specific things you can do:

1. Stop spending and, where you have to spend, look for savings.

2. Increase your skills to become corporate indispensable, rewarded by a higher salary, to increase the amount you can put aside.

When you achieve these two things, you will see the light of financial freedom, probably not experienced since your first wages. By reducing your spending and, at the same time, increasing your income you are expanding your 'earned disposable income' (EDI).

In contrast, if you stay in the working trap you may earn more as a natural progression reaches promotion but you will also spend more. Higher income is paid for higher responsibility and more stress in equal measures. You will reward that higher stress and responsibility with a bigger house, a more expensive car and certainly more expensive holidays. It is no coincidence that higher management get more days off.

Don't get me wrong. There is absolutely nothing wrong with owning a house, driving a smart car, having a lovely and enjoyable family and taking plenty of holidays. It's actually what makes us all happy. But don't suffer at work as a trade-off for this, and don't overspend to make it all feel worthwhile.

Being self-employed isn't necessarily the way to a better life, either. Many people who have stayed in the corporate sector have climbed the working ladder and are very wealthy though. Let's take a look at the Chief Executive Officers (CEO) of the UK's FTSE top 100 companies. An analysis by Robert Half suggests that

> 'internal promotions to CEO positions are on the rise, representing 70% of new CEO appointments in the last year, and nearly half (46%) of CEOs overall. Furthermore, 15% of current FTSE 100 CEOs have spent their entire careers with the same company, a figure that has risen every year since 2015 when the number stood at only 7%.'[18]

The point is, you can use work to generate a life you want by making sure you spend less and increase your salary more, thus creating high levels of EDI. You would think the CEO of a FTSE 100 company would be wealthy. They will undoubtedly command a hefty salary but what are they doing with that income? High salaries may appear to be an automatic route to wealth, but many waste them on elaborate spending and poor investments, not on the moderate accumulation of slower but certain long-term growth of assets. Whatever work you do, or however high you climb the corporate ladder, you will not be automatically wealthy without sensible financial planning.

My treadmill fears

When I was 26, I was working in the family business. I had been there for nine years, since leaving school. Other than O-Levels I had no professional qualifications. I had fun in those nine years – just maturing, I suppose. I was married with a baby boy and living in the remote countryside in the Lake District.

I made a decent living, had a car, a house (and mortgage) and was happy. I now know I was going through the process with many of my friends, firmly locked into the working trap. It sneaks up! However, I was waking up to the reality that 'this was it'. The family fruit and vegetable supply business was slowly engulfed by the larger supermarkets. Garages began to sell food and other household consumables, and soon even they became our competition. Making a good profit became a problem. Hard work could keep us going, but maybe a significant change was a better solution.

The solution to many in West Cumbria was the same. If business failed, there was always a job at Sellafield, the nuclear power station that sits ominously on the nearby coastline. Working at Sellafield was a target by some and viewed as Easy Street. A suitable place to put in time. I only saw it as a working prison with the bonus of secure pay to waste on fun, cars, things and holidays. There was no way I would end up on that treadmill, hating work that paid well.

Recognising I was in a working trap was not the problem, it was extracting myself from it. I had no decent qualifications, no professional skills other than a Class 1 driving licence; and I didn't fancy forty years behind the wheel of a lorry either. I had a family to support, and the family business was struggling. I decided that I wanted more. I wanted my work to deliver variety, maybe travel, and to experience a fruitful and fuller working life. To achieve this, we sold up, shipped out and went to Edinburgh. I embarked on a short course of study that gave me entry to university and the start of a long journey that eventually led me to financial services.

Today, I love doing what I do. Although you might view it as work, I don't because I am still on my journey to wealth and I see everything I do as working towards that goal. There are plenty of barriers to overcome and, as I did, you can pass them too, but the one barrier you must first overcome is your own attitude.

You are the biggest obstacle to your future happiness and will limit your reach for wealth.

Barriers to our existence appear almost weekly; they can be insurmountable, but only if you let them be. Work would be so dull without such obstacles. Without a doubt, the most enjoyable aspect of the last thirty years has been the struggle. Easy is dull. The feeling and rewards from overcoming a challenge to achieve a successful outcome can be joyous.

The hourly rate time trap

Except for a few CEOs who command enormous salaries, income is constrained by time, too. For example, consider the professional world of accountants and lawyers who charge by the hour for their work, a direct exchange of time at work for money. So, engaging lawyers who charge you £150 per hour will cost you £1,500 for ten hours' work. What the lawyer earns is directly proportional to the time they spend at work, which we know is capped to the maximum available: 168 hours per week, or 8,736 hours per year.

EXAMPLE: LAWYER OR GARDENER?

This lawyer could earn £150 × 8,736 hours per year = £1,310,400.

To achieve this income would require no time for sleep, eating, bathing, rest or play. It is clearly impossible!

In any twenty-four-hour day, we can typically say we sleep for eight hours, travel for one hour, eat and drink three meals taking up two hours, bathe for one hour (say, including toilet time) and we drift for one hour. Drifting is being at work but not being productive, daydreaming. Drifting can be the things you do in the office that cannot be charged to a client account, such as changing an ink cartridge or chatting about the weekend's activity at the coffee machine.

That all adds up to thirteen hours and leaves eleven hours that could be spent on chargeable working time. Over the year, this has now reduced your £1.3 million income to a potential £600,600, working eleven hours solid every day. This lawyer is a workaholic!

Of course, we don't tend to work every day in a week. If you take one full day away you reduce your potential income to £514,800 per annum. When you build in four weeks' holiday and nine bank holidays your potential drops to £460,350. This is still a great income for many, a desirable income, so what is the problem? To remind you, this person charges £150 per hour. They work eleven hours solid per day for six days per week and only rest for Sundays, bank holidays and four weeks' annual leave. If they are not working, they are either travelling, sleeping, eating, bathing or drifting. They have also to ensure at least eleven hours are chargeable at £150 per hour to their clients, every working day.

If you could get this job, you could decide to work for a few years to get the money in early and plentifully, but this money would need to last you for the rest of your life. Currently, in the UK, you would pay 40% tax on most of this income! There would be business expenses to cover too, unless the £150 per hour was your net rate after expenses.

Suppose you are not a highly paid lawyer and instead are a gardener only able to earn £15 per hour. In that case, your real maximum income will be capped at £46,035 per annum. You still pay tax and may have other expenses.

Whether you charge £150 per hour or £15 per hour, it is one hell of a task to become a millionaire, wealthy or even well-off by relying on your salary or charges alone.

In my examples, the lawyer and the gardener both work long hours, leading to burnout. Working even six days per week for eleven hours solid is unsustainable. Both are trading eleven hours for money, every day. Their income depends totally on the rate they charge and the hours they work. They are in the hourly rate time trap.

While I accept that it is possible to work this hard and earn a great income, what happens when the lawyer or the gardener can no longer continue? If they cannot put in the time, they cannot earn. With this working model, no time = no income.

Reducing your time working may be a way to ensure you don't burn out, or lose interest altogether. But that reduces your income, because it reduces your time spent working. Reducing from eleven hours per day to eight hours means you are still busy and working six days per week, but now for 72.7% of the income. Such work-reducing action may lengthen your working lifetime (pushing back your retirement age). But it still has an impact on your net income while you wait to retire, hopefully on a pension – another cost reducing your net income.

The point is, you can love your work and look forward to it, work extremely hard and build a great income too, but for how long is this sustainable? How long can you keep that level of work going to maintain both your income and the lifestyle it supports?

Don't work because you have to

I hope you are starting to build a better reason for working: not just to satisfy your debts and lifestyle but because you realise it is the only opportunity to create wealth for you and your family.

When I was 26, I questioned work. I didn't want to work and explored all the ways to get out of it. I quickly realised the only way out was to work harder and more innovatively, and earn my way out. I needed a job that paid more and, to get it, I needed more knowledge and better qualifications.

My intention, at the time, was to work in a prominent city firm which had excellent prospects for promotion, leading to a better-paid job, secure and with long-term benefits. I had no other principles than that and my understanding was no different from that of many UK workers. It would take me fifteen more years to realise the actual target was to be wealthy.

However, the initial idea is the same. To be wealthy you not only need to work, but also to develop your own skills, to seek promotion and a better income. The more active income, the more investment towards your wealth. You need not just a job, but a secure job. Your employer must want you more than the job that you do. The idea that no one is indispensable is rubbish. While many employees are dispensable, it's the few who are not that employers seek. When you have demonstrated indispensability to your employer, you will have reached the first stage of your future wealth.

Key points

1. Nearly 50% of the UK population is in a savings crisis. Don't be one of them.

2. There has to be a change in the way we think about work and appreciate the income it generates.

3. To be socially mobile, a plan for wealth that relies on luck alone is sheer delusion. Instead make it

plausible by taking the right action and embrace work.

4. It's not just those who hate their job that need to change, but those who love their work, too. You could be on the road to the working trap without knowing.

5. Don't fall into the working trap – credit now, pay later and ever-increasing spending before saving. Get off the treadmill.

6. Stop spending and increase your skills to become corporate indispensable.

7. You cannot reach wealth by simply charging more or working longer hours. You will burn out before you retire.

8. Don't work because you have to, work because you want to.

9. Find a better reason to work than to justify your lifestyle.

10. Your escape route is paved by increasing your EDI and doing something positive with it.

Key message

Whatever your opinion of work, it remains the only certain tool you have as a route to wealth and ultimately out of work. Just having a job is your wealth opportunity. The earlier you realise this, the earlier it will all happen for you.

Key action

Ask yourself this question, 'Are you reliant on your employer, or is your employer reliant on you?' If the first answer is true, then you need to change your attitude and take five steps to ensure you become indispensable to your employer:

1. Get to know the business and the company better.

2. Get to know the people in the company better and the roles they perform.

3. Increase your skills and knowledge to make you the best in your role.

4. Increase your skills, knowledge and qualifications in preparation for the future direction of the business, company or industry.

5. Learn how to manage people, train others and make meaningful presentations to your peers.

2
Political Promises

In December 2019, the UK was in the middle of a general election. The left were promoting give-away treats such as free university education, free prescriptions, free broadband for everyone and a promise of workers' rights and nationalisation to create centrally controlled jobs away from the wealthy of the board room. The right were promising to 'get Brexit done' and a spending spree on infrastructure and job creation, to increase the tax thresholds so you keep more and to increase funding for the NHS to record levels.

The truth is, none of this political tennis really matters. While at age 20, say, you have upwards of sixty-five more years to enjoy a fair, reasonable and affordable life, a UK government can barely last five years. While an individual can achieve a lot in five years, a government cannot.

Each government will make promises but, in reality, what does this mean? Put cynically, it is to meddle with your money and tax, your rights and freedoms, your opportunities and ambitions, your health and your education, your retirement pension and your welfare. It is endless and for the average individual nothing significantly changes.

I want you to take back control, claw free from your government, act independently (within the law) and, above all, take responsibility for your own future. Creating wealth is about creating self-sufficiency first and then spreading the good fortune and wisdom you have created to others.

Suppose you follow my simple work-to-wealth insights and focus everything you do on increasing your personal income, as much as possible and as early as possible. In that case, you won't need to worry about the government: you will be too asset-rich to worry.

The political trap

You cannot turn on the television or any typical mobile device without hearing some political comment, by the government or the opposition. They may be right; they may be wrong.

Political change does little for many people that they could not radically change themselves, without political interventions. I follow politics and have one opinion of them all: we need fewer not more. There is still enough freedom in this country to help yourself.

Thinking that a change in politics will be your saviour is the political trap. If you end up in this trap or any version of the working trap, you have no control of your money or your future. You need to know about the working trap and the political trap so you can identify them and make personal choices and decisions to avoid them. Along with these traps is the media trap. Echoing my comments about social media in Chapter 1, the media trap is the wider information adults receive from TV and more traditional news messaging. We can all be easily influenced and that is why we must read and gather all the information we need to form our own, educated judgement. Be careful not to rely on another's word alone. Avoid the traps; the truth is difficult to determine. Beware!

The pension trap

In a book about work and wealth, you cannot avoid the word 'pension'. Until now, I have barely mentioned it. The good news is, there are no heavy, factual details about pensions and certainly no recommendation. Briefly, however, allow me to offer a quick explanation so as to set the right tone and the direction in which I wish to take you.

A pension is designed to replace your income when you retire and, in the UK, available from age 55 (this used to be age 50). Prior to age 55, to the average worker a pension is useless. You cannot access it unless you die. Burnout at age 45 cannot, therefore, be easily supported by a pension. In some circumstances of ill health some pensions can be taken earlier but these are tightly defined.

No government since the early 1960s has had a term in office without meddling with pension provision. This is why a whole industry of financial advisers exists. You see, pensions are a source of tax control for the government. First, they entice you to save, with huge tax savings and reliefs, then they reduce the benefits by endlessly adjusting these reliefs to allow them to raise tax revenues. Pensions are already touted to be first in line for the post-COVID-19 tax rises.

Let me be clear. Having stated the political part played in pension provision, pension planning remains a vital part of your journey from work to wealth. Your employer will pay into a pension for you, so take it. But don't rely on it alone and make sure you have other investment and savings strategies in place. Pensions that are well invested will produce annual growth; the growth will depend upon the risk you are willing to take.

Your pension contributions will generally come from working and taxable income, so if you don't put time in at work, you don't get an income or, therefore, a pension. Most working people in the UK today have accepted automatic deductions from their working income to cover tax, National Insurance and now (quite often) a pension contribution.

Think of a pension not as a pot of money, but a deferred income. Instead of taking your income now, you put some money aside and take it after age 55, when three-quarters of it is taxed as earned income, at the tax rates at that time. If you rely on your pension, politicians control when and how much of your money in that pension you can access. We have to have pensions, simply because of their tax advantages, so set one up, maximise the contribution and then plan the rest of your finances as if you don't have one.

I am not saying don't save into a pension. You may need the pension income in your retirement. I am attempting to persuade you to work for another reason than just income now and pension later. I want you to understand and monitor your progress to a wealthier life that is not reliant on income now combined with pension income at retirement, as this places too much reliance on political promises. Wealth can buy you freedom from political promises.

I work, I have a pension, I am settled

Suppose you have a good job and you pay into a pension set up for you through your employer. Your job will occupy you until your late 60s and the pension you save into each month is targeted to replace your lost income when you retire. Superb! Job done!

You're not wealthy though, are you? For starters, there are restrictions to the amount you can contribute into a pension and the overall value you can hold before tax penalties arise. You have settled again. You have a job you like, you are happy with the income you receive, your retirement looks sorted too. You holiday, you enjoy weekends with friends and family and life is good. Yes? So why are you reading this book?

The pension trap is an extension to the working trap, only less obvious. A pension will accumulate over time and the projections you receive year on year show your potential retirement income based upon standard rates of growth that the whole industry uses. The projection assumes your contributions continue into the future. It might look good or bad, but it's hard to understand that so many of us pop our annual pension statement in a drawer and wait to see what it looks like next year. Is this you?

Conversely, if things are too good, complacency could lead you to struggle; we all need change and action. If your employer is contributing 5%, 6% or even 10%

into your pension and you like the work and pay, why would you seek anything else? This is a sign that you have settled for the pension trap. I have heard people say, 'The job is only OK, but it's a good pension.'

A helpful way of thinking about pension saving is to see the pension contributions for each working week as being intended to pay for the equivalent week once you retire. (If you look at the section in Chapter 7 on compound interest, you'll see that this is greatly over-simplified.) The point is, if you don't earn for a week, you have lost two weeks' income, one now and one in retirement.

There is nothing wrong with a pension plan. Everyone should have one; the problem is it needs your attention. How much you get out depends on how much you put in. Consider this, though: retirement is reserved for those who work; the wealthy do not retire. Just be aware of the different traps.

Politicians, family and friends make poor mentors

There is another reason why people fall into these traps of life. They listen to the wrong people and even seek advice from the wrong people. When people find out what I do, they soon start to tell me about their finances and how they know someone in my industry. I instantly know their financial provision is weak and the person they are talking about is probably not their paid financial adviser, and often not a financial adviser at all but someone who appears financially astute.

How do I know this? Because they are in the pension trap, pleased to tell me they have one. They are quietly trying to get my confirmation that it's a good scheme, feeding their need for reassurance. People act this way with many things. When people are unsure about something, they tell you what they are doing and, since we usually don't want to upset them, we nod and reassure them.

Stop seeking reassurances and taking advice about your finances from friends, family and colleagues – or worse, politicians – because you are being guided by the wrong mentors. Personally, I prefer to listen to real achievers like Grant Cardone. Grant is described on Amazon as 'a *New York Times* bestselling author, the #1 sales trainer in the world, and an internationally renowned speaker on leadership, real estate investing, entrepreneurship, social media and finance'. His five privately held companies have annual revenues exceeding $100 million.[19] He talks a lot about people in the working trap and how they are locked into a predetermined route in life: first education, then work, then retirement. He says that people who accept this life have 'given up'. He means they have settled for what is in front of them.

Stop spending, start saving and investing

The good news is, you are saving into a pension, bene-fiting from tax deference and tax-efficient growth and (by choice or otherwise) getting used to having less in your pocket and something in savings; less to spend, might be a better way to put it. If so, have you noticed how easy it is to adjust your spending to allow for your contribution to your new pension? This helps build up to the next matter to address.

Now that you know how easy it is to save into a pen-sion, it is just as easy to set up another savings plan, like the pension but more flexible. I hear you say, 'I cannot afford another savings plan!' Then you now need to stop spending. Before you spend anything simply ask yourself: 'Do I need this?' The chances are, you don't.

Take Amazon. They have grown revenue from $0 in 1997 to an estimated $488 billion for 2021 and most of the stuff they sell is not truly needed.[20] Ironically, you may have purchased this book from Amazon.

There is no such thing as 'shopping for wealth', but there are 'wealth shoppers'. The order is clear. Unless you already have wealth don't go shopping. I will define my measure of wealth in Part Two, but for now and for the purpose of this message, you're not yet wealthy enough to shop whenever you feel like it. Stopping spending is the first step to saving.

Cash is not king, but cashflow is

Now, don't get confused here. If you do stop spending unnecessarily, you will of course retain more of your income. That's a good thing. The mistake is to then think storing up cash is the same as saving.

Saving, like work, has two meanings relevant to finances:

- You can save by spending less on something: a bargain.

- You can save by putting money into a bank account or other investment.

Be warned, paying less on a purchase is only a saving if you truly needed the item in the first place. If you need a new washing machine because the old one is broken then, if the machine is normally £300 and you get it for £200, you have indeed saved £100. However, it is only a true saving if the £100 that you avoided spending is then placed into an investment. If, instead, you spend the £100 on something you don't need – a new sports bag, for example, when the one you have is fine – then you've saved nothing.

Remember cashflow. This is the money that flows through your bank account. Keep a sensible emergency fund, but then accumulate cashflow by directing money above what you need for that fund into a better investment than a bank account.

CASE STUDY: FINANCIAL DIFFICULTIES

I met a couple, Nicola and Paul, in financial difficulty. Both had jobs, they owned a house and they had two children. All should have been fine, but their spending had gone out of control. They not only had a mortgage at 90% of their house value, but over £30,000 of debts. They had no monetary savings at all. They were totally reliant on their weekly income to survive day to day. They asked for my help.

When I gathered all their financial information, I discovered three major and typical financial blunders:

1. **Deferred purchases** – At £27,000 of debt, they arranged a new central heating system at a cost of £3,000 because the seller offered a 'free period': buy now pay next year.

2. **Luxuries, not needs** – They had direct debits for Sky, contact lenses, gym membership and mobile phones, because they classed these and other luxuries as needs.

3. **No budget planning** – Their monthly outgo exceeded their monthly income by £500 because they bought on impulse, and failed to assess affordability. They had no emergency funding.

The first action was to reduce the outgo to below the income. This was tough. First, we cancelled all luxury direct debits – Sky, gym membership – and converted mobile phones to pay-as-you-go. I took a look at their food bill and discovered they regularly ordered take-out food. Clothes were bought new, not second-hand. Changes were necessary.

Next, we tackled their use of credit, contacting each credit card provider to reduce the outgo and merge to a lower rate where we could. All were cut up and they switched to using cash only.

This may sound harsh, but they were in real trouble and action was needed. We managed to squeeze their outgo below their income, finding great financial relief.

Once their outgo was below their net income, they had to sustain this until the first of their debts was clear in just a few years. I urged them to work overtime, or find a second income stream until they had reduced all debts.

They now had a plan to rid themselves of their debt without the need for bankruptcy or an individual voluntary arrangement. The biggest threat to this was whether they could continue to hold their jobs down. After the presentation of my plan to this couple, they stated two things that have stuck in my mind to this day:

- 'Thank you so much, it's been so stressful and now this is sorted we can book a restful holiday in the sun.'
- 'The Government should do something to help people in our situation, having two children and a threat of redundancy.'

The working trap and the political trap at work.

Debt – a very common problem

The Money Charity reports on their website (for March 2021) that UK debt per household is £61,435, made up of both secured and unsecured debts:[21]

Type of personal debt	Total UK personal debt	Per household
Secure mortgages	£1,516.2 billion	£54,397
Unsecured consumer debt	£196.7 billion	£7,057
(of which credit card)	(£54.2 billion)	(£1,945)
Grand total (March 2021)	£1,712.9 billion	£61,435

Significantly, unsecured debt is debt which there are no assets to offset, and the figure of £7,057 is *per household*. The figure *per adult* is £3,712, which is more than twice the average net monthly income per adult.

This all converts to the reason why the majority of individuals work: because they have to! They have no assets that are not covered by debts and little to no savings. They rely on the working income and it is spent the moment they receive it.

Don't let this be you.

Key points

1. Individuals must take back control of their own destiny and not rely on others, especially politicians.

2. Everyone should save in a pension scheme, especially if available through your employer.

3. Governments always meddle with pensions tax rules and benefits, so pensions are not something to rely on.

4. Once you have set up a pension, consider the rest of your financial planning as if the pension does not exist.

5. Having a good job and a good pension does not mean you are on the road to being wealthy.

6. Don't take advice from media, politicians, family or friends just because they mean well. Take advice *only* from professionals in their field.

7. Politicians, family and friends can make poor mentors.

8. Stop spending, start saving and investing.

9. Cash is not king, cashflow is.

10. Avoid debt accumulation, it's easy to fall into.

Key message

Politics looks like it might make a difference to your life and for some there is satisfaction in seeing political change; however, change rarely affects the wealthy. They are so protected by their own fortune that failed promises come and go without having any significant impact on their own plans.

Key action

Make sure you have maximised your pension contribution through your employer or that you are paying into one if you are self-employed. An independent financial adviser can help you. See 'Your Call to Action' at the end of this book.

3

Active And
Passive Income

So far, I have explained the traps you face in a typical working life that is born from the education you received. They are traps because, once in them, once these processes of social media imagination, work dependency, pension and political reliance enfold you, to rid yourself of these burdens requires three things:

1. Increasing and investing your working (active) income

2. Understanding (passive) income and how it is generated

3. Having willpower to change in the pursuit of an enjoyable working life

I will address your determination to change in Chapter 5, but first I need to continue to build your path to understanding the reasons for this and prepare you to see your current life as a trap unless you know how to address it.

In this chapter I aim to address factors 1 and 2. and explain the difference between active and passive income. You probably don't yet realise it, but your aim is to work towards having a passive income.

Employees work to generate an income, through salary, wages or some paid event under a contract. This income is directly related to the work they do, and I class it as 'active' income. They have to be active to achieve that income. If they are not active, then they do not generate any income.

This means they have to work even if they don't want to. They have bills to pay and other such commitments. No work, no income. It's the position almost everyone will be in, especially during the early years of their working life.

Big field

When you sleep (or lie awake worrying about money, maybe) you are probably resting from a hard day's work. You may do physically tiring work, or a less physical white-collar job that is also exhausting.

Meeting after meeting, long discussions, notes and reports to write and present, client concerns to address, manager deadlines to meet, diaries and planning to sort out – the day is sometimes endless and the job, when all matters are addressed and targets achieved, simply starts again the next day and this continues on, and on.

But what if you could earn while you sleep? This is what the landed gentry and their ancestors have been doing for years.

Let's say you own land and rent it to local farmers. The rent they pay you is passive income, because it lands in your bank without you needing to work on the land to make it. The farmers are working, not you. No boss, no hours at work, no targets, no training, no stress: you just own the land. Further, the bigger the fields, the larger the rental income from the farmer. So long as the farmer rents the field from you, you will have a passive income.

Adopt the mentality of the landed gentry

I am sure you will have heard the term 'landed gentry' but do you know exactly what it means and where it came from?

The landed 'gentry' is described as 'a largely historical British social class consisting of landowners who could live entirely from rental income, or at least had a country estate'.[22] Such lands passed down to the first-born only, while daughters and younger sons inherited cash or stocks, and comparatively small amounts.

OK, I accept you are unlikely to inherit a large country estate with tenant farmers to pay you rent but this does not mean you cannot aim for even a small portion of that outcome. Instead of an estate, consider owning commercial property. Instead of farmers, consider a small business paying you rent. A tasty apple is still tasty whether the bite you take is big or small. The important thing to remember is that someone started something and ended up with a country estate; you can do the same.

You will of course have to work first, to earn the income to invest towards owning such grandeur. A bite at a time.

The agricultural depression in the 1870s saw the landed gentry begin to decline, though many still own and rent out land today. These once vast inherited estates are fewer and further between, others sold to investors, instead of passing by inheritance alone. Land is now readily available to anyone. Therefore, if you have the resources, you can acquire land to rent and with it a passive income.

Unfortunately, most of the UK population appear to think that unless an inheritance is expected, or a lottery windfall, they have to work for an (active) income forever. 'I have to work because I have nothing and therefore I have no choice' or 'I work because I have to'.

Wealth is available to everyone, not just the fortunate

Of course, you can create the drive and ambition to own land. If you want a passive income from land, then you need to buy land. If no inheritance or windfall is due, you will have to earn the money to buy it with. So here we are again: you have to work 'actively' to generate the income and spend little of it until you have saved enough to buy land.

Nearly everyone in the UK will know about this process, when they connect it to the ownership of your own home. It's usually the first big purchase the average person makes and requires a big mortgage, up to 90% of the purchase price. The average mortgage in the UK is over £130,000 with a typical repayment term of twenty-five years.[23] The owners of these mortgages will work hard to pay them off; some manage to do this earlier than the original loan term. The problem is, this house and the land it sits on will generate no income because you have to live in it. It is therefore a huge investment and commitment that will generate you no passive income. It's part of the working trap.

Most people argue that, if they pay off their mortgage, they will have more disposable income saved from the monthly mortgage payments. What if you never pay off the mortgage but, as the property value grows over time, you borrow more to buy more properties?

My first mortgage was for a house valued at £30,000. I could buy that in one go today. That same house is worth £150,000 today, thirty-three years later. I remember struggling to pay that mortgage, as many do every month. Now it seems daft. The house has grown in value by £120,000 and if I had not changed my life's direction and stayed in that house all this time, doing the same job, I would have failed to utilise that £120,000 equity.

Your home is an asset – use it. Use the growth to fund other projects. It's what the wealthy have done and it's easy. I will cover more of this in Chapter 8, but for now know this. If you work, you have access to wealth. If you have a mortgage, you have access to wealth. If you are educated, you have access to wealth. Opportunity is around you, in touching distance, you just cannot see it.

So far I have mentioned work, land and home. These are all things that have a value to you. All either generate cash or can be converted into cash. They are also known as 'assets'. Assets are the resources owned by a person or a business.

Consider the big field rented to a farmer again. The field is an asset. If you own the land, then you own the asset. It has value. You could sell it for cash. You could rent it out and gain an income. If you do not own the land, you do not own the rental income.

Income follows assets (follow income)

In 2015 I wanted to boost the income to my business and was unsure exactly which direction to go. Although I had built a good business over the five years before, I felt that I had reached the limit of my ability and I needed more knowledge in business to progress further. I set about searching for new information on business growth. I read books, watched videos, searched Google for snippets of inspiration and made enquiries to those I felt could help me. To my astonishment, nothing jumped out. All information I already had in some form or another. Then I came across a book called *Key Person of Influence* by Daniel Priestley.[24]

This book led me to the 'entrepreneur journey', which was a short study of businesses from start-up to greater than £50 million turnover. It so matched my journey in business to date, I had to embark on this new journey and I signed up to Daniel's nine-month programme. It was intense. There was so much information to take in. However, one short phrase changed my view not only of my business and the way I was growing it, but the way I was to run my own personal finances and life. It was always there, I just needed confirmation from someone who was already seeing the benefits of his work. That phrase was 'income follows assets', ie to achieve an income you first need an asset. This was my first moment of epiphany. I realised that all I needed was to accumulate assets. It's what you need to do, too.

I was already investing in stock markets, and I was already developing property, but I had not realised that this was accumulating assets. My epiphany was connecting what I was already doing to the notion that accumulating assets is essential to achieve wealth, specifically assets that generate income.

To expand this, I needed to save more money in the right areas to generate more assets. I decided to invest in my own company. In fact, Daniel has since written about business requiring at least twenty-four assets to maximise opportunity. I will cover business in Part Two but, needless to say, the phrase 'income follows assets' as a general approach to creating wealth has changed my approach to everything. No asset = no passive income!

I have developed this idea further since first encountering it because, although it lends itself well to business growth and the entrepreneur journey, it does not fit well with the average employee in the UK, since they have control over only one main asset: themselves – at first, certainly.

Few people think of themselves as assets. The number one asset to any start-up business is the owner of that business. When you think about it, if you work you generate an income and if income follows assets, then you are an asset.

Equally, an employee is an asset to an employer. Unfortunately, some employers don't realise their employees are assets, adding to the employer's own growth potential. As an employee you help generate income, and income follows assets!

There is a problem with 'income follows assets' though. The phrase means passive income, like the rental income from a big field. However, to grow assets you first need active (earned or working) income. I have therefore added a first step to allow for the accumulating of assets generated from working income, so 'income follows assets' becomes 'income follows assets (follow income)'.

Investing active income ▶ accumulates assets ▶ passive income

Income ◀ follows assets ◀ follow income

So what do we know?

- We know that (passive) income comes from assets.

- We know that assets grow after (active) income is invested and it grows.

To simplify these phrases into a more directive term I have coined the word 'assetise'. The word explains what you need to do with your active working income.

Assetise your income

From now on, you need to stop spending and start saving into a regular investment plan. If you need to know what investment plan, then you should seek independent financial advice. I talk about this in Chapter 10.

Assetise your income = convert active income into passive income

These regular investments may at first be small, perhaps £100 to £300 per month initially, but they soon accumulate over time. If you work hard and develop your working skills, you could earn a promotion and, rather than spend the increased salary, continue living on the income you have been accustomed to and instead increase your regular investments. Small and regular is investing, too. By investing regularly, you are growing an asset that one day will be big enough to be a deposit on a property or business venture, or both.

It takes a while to get going but, at some point, the momentum kicks in and you will see the benefits.

Active income

Let's say that, like many people in the UK, you have little or no savings and maybe even run a small unsecured debt on a credit card. You would say you have no assets. You may be in the working trap I described in Chapter 1 and just starting to realise you need to do something about your situation. You may be saying, 'That's all very well, Andrew, but how do I start from scratch?'

Firstly, you are the biggest and best asset you have. You produce an income from employment. So, if you want to stop working and still draw an income you need other assets beside yourself. These other assets will all come from your active working income; your assets will grow over time and, as they do, they start to produce passive income. You might not be able to buy land for many years, but you can certainly receive a passive income from savings. For example, interest from a bank account is passive income. A sum of £1,000 in a savings account will generate little interest in today's low-interest-rate society, but it is still a passive income. If you are happy to take a little more risk, investing this same £1,000 may produce a small passive income: I discuss risk and return in Chapter 7.

Of course, the best way to grow your assets quickly is to reinvest the passive income too and compound the growth so both the original investment and the passive income grow.

Passive income

Until now you have only had active income to think about. You work and then spend your working income. You may save something but it is typically set for some future spend. Imagine there was a rule forbidding you from spending active income on anything other than absolute living essentials and only allowing you to buy non-essentials with passive income.

This rule would mean you can have a holiday but spend no more on it than income that is passive; none of the active income you receive for working. Wow!

Now, you might think that ridiculous, but this is happening today. Once just about anyone could buy a home, but today house prices have grown so much they have priced out the younger generation. The rule is, if you want to own your own home you have to have at least £20,000 to deposit. You can hope to inherit that deposit or you can save it from earned income.

EXAMPLE: INCOME FOLLOWS ASSETS FOLLOW INCOME

If your holiday cost you £2,000 and rental from a property you own was £8,000 after all expenses, then under the rules above, you could take that holiday.

Imagine instead this property was mortgaged. Let's say the value was £200,000 and you paid a £20,000 deposit (10% equity in that property). The regular rental yield is 4%, giving 4% × £200,000 = £8,000 as stated above; but the mortgage payment is 3% × £200,000 = £6,000. You could still afford the holiday:

- Rental income   =   £8,000
- *Less* Mortgage payment   =   (£6,000)
- Passive income   =   £2,000

See how easy it is to generate a passive income. You have had to save £20,000 deposit (plus any expenses, stamp duty, tax and legal costs), gain a mortgage, purchase a property that you rent – and you have a passive income.

A word of warning. This is for illustration purposes, to show the principles of how passive income can be generated. At this point your income still relies on your ability to work. You are nowhere near ready to live passively. Equally, it is unlikely a lender would allow you to buy for the purpose of renting a property without a 25% deposit. I am deliberately simplifying to show the principles of building wealth from work.

Work is the process of exchanging time for earnings. You need to turn your current working active income into assets that in turn produce a passive income. When you generate passive income, the door to wealth widens. The secret is to not spend all your earned income and use the money to fund asset growth.

If you earn £1,000 and spend £1,000, then you have nothing left. If you earn £1,000 and spend £600, then the £400 you save will produce an income for you if assetised. It's not a difficult idea to grasp but it is difficult to achieve because of social pressures and the common need to find reward for hard work.

In contrast, for the rich, income and wealth are different. They rarely receive active income; instead, they rely on 'passive' income. Passive income comes from assets (capital) which they own or in which they have an interest. Even if that asset is not yet owned (because they have borrowed to buy it), they still draw passive income from it. These income-producing assets do the work for you and may not require you to invest much (perhaps any) time in them.

Asset delegation

The wealthy are comfortable managing people and taking charge. This is delegation and part of any business owner's drive for growth is to hire staff and delegate tasks. This creates both a job for the employee and wealth for the owner. Delegation is something they have to learn and do well.

When the years of building the business are over and they have wealth, they continue to delegate to people other than business staff now. The wealthy have housekeepers, cooks and gardeners, to name a few. But the wealthy also delegate to assets.

To prepare you for Chapter 4 (Asset Accumulation), the wealth creator delegates the task of growing assets (to generate income) by investing, because they know assets will create more wealth, more certainly, than their own labour.

For many people with limited resources, accumulating assets may appear a distant challenge, even unachievable. I can hear the defeatist thinking – 'I don't have any money' or 'I don't earn enough'. The good news is, you don't have to do anything other than change your mindset. Each day on your way to work, repeat these five simple rules:

1. I do not work to waste time.

2. I do not work to spend.

3. I do not work to save.

4. I do not work because I have to.

5. I work for money to invest, to accumulate assets.

Now that you have established the need for a passive income in exchange for a life of working for a living, you must change your working week from generating an active income to one that will ultimately build assets to generate a passive income.

Key points

1. Ridding yourself of social media imagination, work dependency, pension and political reliance requires:

    a. The knowledge to generate and grow your working income,

    b. The understanding of passive income, where it comes from and how to generate it, and

    c. Determination to change.

2. Adopt the mentality of the landed gentry, who live entirely from passive income.

3. Wealth is available to everyone, not just the fortunate.

4. Income follows assets, follow income. So, assetise your income.

5. The wealthy delegate to people, and they also delegate to their assets.

6. Over time, assets create more wealth than labour.

Key message

You must understand the difference between active earned income and passive income that comes from assets. It's fundamental to your wealth creation. When you start investing, you are delegating the task of accumulating assets to your asset partner. The two of you are growing *your* wealth together in the same time frame. While you work, your investments are working too.

Key action

Take a blank piece of paper, position it landscape and draw two columns. In one column, list your active income from working. In the second, write down the passive income from assets you own. Add them up and see which generates the greatest and which the least income. Your target (for now) is for your passive income to equal the active income, the difference is how far you currently fall short of hitting that target.

Since an asset can typically produce a 4% income yield, then to find the assets value you need to accumulate, multiply the difference (shortfall) by twenty-five and that gives you the target value. This works because 4% is 4 parts per 100 and 4 can be written as $100/25$ giving the formula $4 \times 25 = 100$. (Similarly, if you are confident you could achieve 5% income yield, then since $5 \times 20 = 100$, to find the assets value you need to accumulate, multiply by twenty.)

4
Asset Accumulation

In earlier chapters, you learned that to be financially self-sufficient you need to adopt a different reason to work and not rely on political interventions to save or help you. Work itself does not need to change at the outset, but your approach and rationale for working does. Put simply, you should work for income and not for a living.

You also learned that you need to convert your working income into assets, to assetise your income.

When you work, your income should be working too

When you realise that working for a living is a dead end, then you see that working for an income is the start of an accumulation of assets. If you earn £100 and only spend £80, you have £20. The secret is to treat that £20 as capital and not something to spend. If that £20 was a share of a property (for example) and that property produced a rental income to you of 4% per annum, that same £20 would produce 80p. That 80p is a passive income from a £20 property asset.

All you need now is more of these assets – thousands of them if you save £20 at a time, but I choose this figure to show that 'every penny counts'. Therefore, before you decide it's too daunting a task, ask your-self whether you would walk past a £20 note if it were lying in the street. Would you? Get used to the idea of working for income that you will change into assets. Think of working as mining for money.

In this chapter, I aim to distinguish the types of assets and specify those you should aim to accumulate. Desirable assets are 'income-producing assets' or IPAs: busy assets that work for you. Easy to remember if, like me, you like a beer!

One asset works harder for you than any other, and it is probably the most important asset of all: you. In Chapter 1, I suggested you should become a great asset to your employer, indispensable to the firm. This puts you in control of your future. I also stated that 15% of the CEOs of FTSE 100 companies have risen through the company they started working in.[25] They became so indispensable to the firm that they became the obvious choice for the highest staff position, CEO.

As an asset, you produce an income, which makes you an IPA. Given support, the ability to learn and, at times, luck, you could become a valuable IPA. That sounds good, but the point of this book is to move you away from being the only IPA you possess and instead to harness your power to produce income to create other IPAs, until your passive income exceeds your active income.

The secret to holding the right assets is to find and treat an asset as if it is a valued employee. Put the asset to work. An asset that does not produce an income is not working.

Types of assets

The three main 'passive' IPAs are investments, property and business. Each may seem more inaccessible than the one before. In Part Two I will show you how to start accumulating assets through investing in stocks and shares, while using your home to help you accumulate property assets. For the brave and entrepreneurial the accumulation of business assets is equally rewarding.

When accountants talk about assets, they categorise them into three basic groups:

- Liquid or illiquid (fixed) assets

- Tangible or intangible assets

- Operating or non-operating assets

If you talk to a financial adviser, they will categorise assets as:

- Shares

- Bonds

- Property

- Commodities

- Cash

Both accountants and IFAs are right. Which categorisation to use depends on what we are trying to achieve. The accounting categories cover just about everything and group them according to their tax treatment, accessibility or value. In contrast, the financial adviser is more concerned with risk to their client's capital. For the time being, I want you to focus on four asset groups around you:

- You = active income

- Your investment = passive income

- Your property = passive income

- Your business = first active, later passive income

These are IPAs, the means to build your wealth. Accountants' or financial advisers' definitions don't tell you what will build your wealth. Classic cars, oil paintings, fine wine, stamps, furniture or other chattels are nice once you are wealthy, but they don't produce an income.

Empty assets

The asset that is hardest to value fairly is your home. When you buy a house to live in, you are told it's the most important and largest purchase you will make. You are prepared to buy it over twenty-five or thirty years, which may be the rest of your working life. However, when you do pay off the mortgage, you will own an asset that is not an IPA. You live in this house, so how can it produce an income for you? You can argue that ownership removes the need to pay rent or a mortgage, so has the same effect as producing an income. This may have the same effect, but is not the same thing: no actual income is generated so I class this as an empty asset.

If you want to be wealthy, I believe you should use a mortgage to buy your first house, but see it as a step to build wealth through accumulating property assets, and not try to pay it off. Your first property purchase should be your main home. This has many tax advantages, but never selling it maximises these. Once bought, if you want to move home, buy another and rent the old house. Therefore, make sure you buy a house you would subsequently be able to rent.

Avoid empty assets unless they lend themselves to future use. Your home is an empty asset until you buy a second home and rent the first. It will have grown in value but produced no income over that period. It's empty until you fill it with tenants.

The human asset

If you have no money at all and only an income to rely on, then you are the asset. You will always be the foremost income-producing asset and the generator of all other assets. As a human you have the ability to learn and improve yourself, to improve your knowledge, skills and employability. The ability to generate income is the first step. The second step is to increase that income by up-skilling and creating a demand for your abilities. Of course, you need to work to produce income; and ultimately the process to becoming wealthy requires you to continue working, but to generate assets that become IPAs. In short, you won't stop working, but how you work will change.

Double your saving principle

If you save already, have you ever considered what effect doubling your saving would have on your future wealth?

For example, let's pretend you earn £10 per hour. In this tax-free, cost-free world, you need to earn £100. You work for ten hours to earn £100. If you take your pay home and spend it all, you start next week the same way you started this week: broke. However, if in the first working week you spent £99, the left-over £1 could be the first step to building wealth. If you do this a million times, you will become a millionaire. The first problem, however, is time. It will take you 19,230 years to accumulate £1 million this way. Clearly impossible!

So let's move this on. How do we bring the target closer? One answer is to spend £98 and save £2. Doubling your saving will halve the time you need to accumulate £1 million, from 19,230 years to 9,615 years.

This is clearly still impossible, but 44% of us hardly save a thing.[26] It needs to be brought back to the basics. Look at the table below:

Spend	Save	Years to accumulate £1 million
£100	£0	Never
£99	£1	19,230
£98	£2	9,615
£96	£4	4,807
£92	£8	2,403
£84	£16	1,201
£68	£32	600
£36	£64	300

Following the double your saving principle, this table demonstrates how you can reduce the time to accumulate £1 million from 19,230 years down to 300 years. However, the table stops here. You cannot double anymore, since you don't have enough income. Of the £100 you earned, you saved £64 and spent £36. Most people will need at least one-third of their salary or wages to live on.

The answer, therefore, is to earn more!

Earn enough to save

It is essential to drive your knowledge and ability to the highest of your earning potential as an employee. With each salary increase, you then save even more, perhaps even all your increase. Remember, spending will prevent you from becoming wealthy.

Let's give your salary an increase. You have made yourself indispensable at work and have been promoted, now earning £400 per week. You can now double your £64 saving to £128, or even quadruple it:

Spend	Save	Years to accumulate £1 million
£272	£128	150
£144	£256	75

For the first time, you can see a realistic time frame for accumulating £1 million: seventy-five years. You might be able to do this in a lifetime.

Sceptics, please notice that the spend column on the left is now at £144: you are now spending more than 140% of the income you started with and still saving £256. You have achieved this by a combination of increasing your savings and increasing your earnings. Each time you won a pay rise you were able to increase your savings.

Now you have seen this in simple terms you will hopefully be looking for the next pay rise. So here it is: you have been promoted to regional manager and are now earning £400 per week more (£800 per week in total):

Spend	Save	Years to accumulate £1 million
£288	£512	37

You have done it. You have reached a figure to save each week that will allow you to save £1 million in about thirty-seven years. How do you feel? Elated? Probably not, because you have to earn £800 per week and save more than £500. This is more than £2,000 per month to save, over a working life of thirty-seven years.

So the simple 'working/time' model above shows you have reached an *impasse*. What can be done? Instead of saving £512 per week in a box under the bed, you can invest it, effectively putting your working income to work.

Put your money to work

So how do you go about putting your money to work? Consider this. All start-up businesses require money to get them going. Equally, established businesses require money to help them grow. A business makes money by selling something, a service or a product. Services require staff and a product requires manufacture. If the business works well, the initial investment grows in line with the value of the business. Money invested in business works just like an employee. It has value, purpose and a task. Money buys the base materials to build the product for sale. It covers the cost of hiring skilled and experienced staff, and pays their wages. It buys or rents office space. It is the reason there are over 330,000 accountants in the UK, all assessing and reporting on the turnover, gross and net profit of businesses.

So while you may be OK with taking a job from an employer, effectively putting your trust in that person to pay you each month for the work you have put in, why are you so hesitant about investing your money in companies? Think about it. If you are in a company working and making money, why wouldn't you put your money to work in a company, too? When you think it through, it's an obvious concept.

Now expand your thinking and consider this. If you earn £2,000 per month from an employed role in a company, how much would you need to invest in that same company to pay you the same income? The answer, in simple terms, is £600,000.

When a company makes profit (income) this is distributed to the investors (shareholders) who gave the company money to operate with. This distribution is known as dividends. In the UK dividends are typically 4% of an investment's value (some more, some less), so:

(£2,000 × 12 months)/4% dividend = £600,000 investment

So, in this example, you, the employee, are earning £2,000 per month, while the investor who invested £600,000 into the company is also earning £2,000 per month.

There are two important points to note:

1. While you are trading your time for money, the investor is trading little or no time.

2. As the company grows you get no more unless you can negotiate a pay rise, while the £600,000 investment does grow.

Then there is the question of risk. The investor has £600,000 at risk. If the company goes bust, you lose your job, and if your job is your only source of income then you have lost your whole income until you get another job, which is not always easy. However, the investor loses their whole income *and* all their capital!

Sensible investors try to minimise this risk by spreading their investment. Instead of £600,000 invested in one company, what if they invested £10,000 in sixty companies (60 × £10,000 = £600,000)? In this scenario, if the company you work for went bust, you lose your job and your £2,000 per month salary, while the investor loses the £10,000 invested in that company, but retains not only the £590,000 in the other fifty-nine companies but also £1,967 per month income (59/60 × £2,000).

During the COVID-19 pandemic, millions of people lost their jobs across the world. However the stock market only dropped by 20% initially, and has since largely recovered. When a company fails, the staff often lose out before the investors.

When you start life with nothing, all you have is your own ability and you search for work to create money. You trade your time to an employer for an income. But what you do with your income matters more than how much that income amounts to. If you earn £5,000 per month and spend £5,000 per month, you have nothing (except perhaps a few empty assets; and they may rapidly decline in value as you use them). If you earn £2,000 per month and spend only £1,500, you will be £500 per month better off. The skill is to invest that £500 wisely. Invest in companies that you, your friends and family either work for, buy from or know about. You need as little as £50 per month to invest into companies and I will show you in later chapters how to create an investment strategy for your hard-earned saving so you can start to accumulate money, but for now know that you can. I am all about building wealth from certainty, not speculation, so only invest in something you clearly understand.

Asset partners

If you just work, save nothing and build no other assets then you may grow your income but your overall growth will be slower. You need a partner to help you grow. You need another asset. This is why most people go into business with a partner. The idea is that two will grow the business twice as quickly as one. This is another epiphany moment. If you are employed, your business partner is your investment. It is helpful to see your regular investing as your business partner and pay them, too. For example, if you earn £1,000, keep £700 for yourself and give £300 to your asset partner, your regular investment.

As that investment asset grows, it can be used to feed another asset, maybe a business venture asset, which in turn can feed a property asset (a 'buy-to-let' asset, say). In turn each asset funds the next asset until you have a portfolio of assets across the four main groups I mentioned in 'Types of assets' above.

Every wealthy person I meet, read about or follow recognises that the number one asset is themselves. Number two is to spend little, learn to save and invest regularly to build a portfolio of accessible capital. The third asset is to use the accessible capital for deposits to acquire mortgages and buy land and property to rent. The fourth asset is the business they are in; whether employed or self-employed, they ensure they are great at what they do.

If you know anything about driving or riding a bike, you will know that setting off in top gear is extremely difficult and sometimes impossible; you stall. You need to get going first, so you use a lower gear to help you do this. Once moving, you select a higher gear and keep doing this until you've selected the gear that is best for where you want to go.

Accumulating assets is the same. Gear one is you. Get yourself going and increase your ability to earn more by self-improvements. The more you earn, the more you can invest. When the investments start to grow, you move into second gear. Continue to grow the income and, in turn, this higher income feeds the investments, and they grow too. As you improve, your investments grow, both working together. Soon you will move into gear three. This is where you use some of the investment you have accrued to fund major investments, like property or whole companies. Again, like the accumulated investments, you accumulate property or businesses to rent and, where necessary, repair and recycle. Now there are three assets all working together. Gear four is where you have built a business that generates so much passive income that you can use that income to fund future investments, property, or other businesses, as appropriate.

Eventually, you reach a point where you can move out of that generative gearing, leaving the investment, property and businesses to fund each other while you, with your new-found skills, move onto higher-level business development, mergers and acquisitions in search of even bigger money mines.

Key points

1. Think of working as mining for money.

2. The desirable assets are income-producing assets (IPAs).

3. Think of your assets as employees, so put them to work.

4. An empty asset is one that produces no income.

5. If the first asset you buy is your main home, try renting it if or when you move; that way, it will transition from an empty asset to an IPA.

6. Earn enough to invest. If you aim to double your savings, you will need to double your income at some point. Time is not on your side so don't hesitate.

7. Put your money to work. If you are an employee, you rely on that business being a success, so spread your risk by investing in other businesses.

8. While you work trading time for money, the investor trades little or no time but can earn passively what you earn actively.

9. Keep asset accumulation simple, working with just four main groups: you, your investment, your property and your business.

10. Only invest in assets that you understand.

Key message

Without a windfall, wealth comes from work alone. To accumulate wealth, you first need to earn enough to invest. I have shown that you cannot work your way to wealth on time alone. You can, however, earn more, which will allow you to save more and so invest more. The principle 'income follows assets' is succeeded by 'assets follow income'.

Key action

Without referring to the book or any notes you have taken, explain to your partner, spouse, friend or colleague the different asset classes and how you can make money from them. Explain what makes your home an empty asset and how it can become an IPA. Explain passive and active income and why you are the main asset to start your asset accumulation journey. Get them on your journey with you.

5
Meaningful Change

I have been accused by many people of 'always changing my mind'. To them it's a frustration, to me it's making progress.

I recall a joiner fitting doors and windows in our house who complained to me about having to remove and change the doors he had just fitted. It's not that I was unhappy with his work, or the doors, but having seen the outcome, I decided changes were needed. I could not see his problem; after all, I was still paying him.

Having completed the joinery work he felt he had done his job, yet ensuring the client was satisfied had not been part of his goal. Goals are small gains you achieve on the way towards an ultimate target and my target was not just to have new doors fitted. It was to ensure the whole house and garden was not only comfortable to live in but a pleasant and rewarding visual experience.

When you look at the most wonderful buildings in the world, such as Westminster Abbey, Château Frontenac in Canada and the unusual Flatiron Building in New York, all involved attention to detail and constant change in response to challenges during construction. We seem to accept that important and expensive projects require detail and fuss, but for some reason assume a simple door in a house in some Scottish village is not so important.

Change requires desire, courage and perseverance

If you truly want to be wealthy, you have to make meaningful changes to your attitude towards work and what you do with the money you earn. Such prosperity does not come easy. Meaningful change to your life requires setting goals, thinking big and then finding a way to achieve those goals by taking the first step. You have to be prepared to give something up. The desire to be wealthy is not enough, you need courage and perseverance too, in significant chunks. If you currently spend everything you earn and think a switch to investing £100 per month is meaningful change, then you are mistaken. It is a start, a change, yes, but just that. Meaningful change is about doing different things, not doing the same thing differently; it requires a significant change to the mindset before anything else and this change always starts with denial. Small changes only appease your desires, they don't achieve them.

COVID-19 – forced change

Between 1918 and 1920 the Spanish flu killed possibly as many as 100 million people worldwide. This was followed by six long years of recovery both from the First World War and this pandemic.[27] During these years the Roaring Twenties began. In 1924 the stock market began rising. It increased in value by 20% a year and the number of shares traded doubled to 5 million per day.[28]

Armed with this information, it is plausible that in our future years, after the current coronavirus pandemic, change is inevitable. People's attitude towards money will change. The way people think about life will change; priorities will change. There will be good years and bad years. Expect a turbulent decade, so prepare for change.

If you are still in denial about your own need to make changes, it's because change brings worry, so it's natural for you to resist. To make no changes and hope, in the light of past experience, is a futile act of self-reassurance. If you really want better than you have, you need to be prepared to change, embrace it then endure it.

Viewing change as a good thing, a catalyst for self-analysis and maybe self-sufficiency, then change is welcome. In fact, you start to let go and search for new challenges. Change should always be a positive thing. Let's face it, the coronavirus was not your fault, nor the fault of the financial markets. It's a change that was dumped upon you, upon us. The key to success is to look for the opportunities, ride the waves of realisation for a while and then put in place meaningful changes to ensure you float while others sink.

I love change. I have changed house four times in the last eight years, I have changed my car four times in the last five years, I often change my mind but, every time I change, I make a slight improvement. It may cost me in time and resources, but there are benefits. I change because I am constantly searching for better, for improvement and for opportunity. Sometimes change is two steps back, in order to be able to make three forward.

Resolutions without fear

Resolutions occur to most of us every New Year. It is a time when we all give ourselves a new start and aim to dump the old, bad habits. We might give up alcohol through January, stop smoking, plan to lose weight, exercise more and, for the few, plan our finances better. But these resolutions never last long, do they?

The problem is not the desire to change, it is the lack of real commitment. To effect real and meaningful change to your lifestyle, for the better, takes more than a desire or a vision of what better looks like. It takes energy, drive and ambition. For resolutions to stick there also needs to be some fear of failure. Resolutions without fear do not work. People give up smoking because they fear cancer. Failed resolutions come from an underlying tendency, when the pressure is on, to convince yourself that being you as you are now is fine. You are comfortable with your life really and only desire suggests you want more. Having a resolution and failing to carry it out completely means you can at least say 'you tried'. The world is full of dreamers but lacks achievers.

I don't do New Year resolutions anymore because they are meaningless and only serve to deny my personal failings for a while. For example: I enjoy a drink, so stopping for a month in January is pointless. If you start to drink again in February then, apart from feeling fitter for a month, overall nothing meaningful has been achieved. Change must be permanent to be meaningful. To keep the example going, an alcoholic must stop drinking permanently and never take even a single drink, if they want a longer and healthier life.

When you become wealthy, you will fear losing that wealth. Maintaining wealth is why many successful people keep going. They fear a drift back to the old ways. Like the alcoholic example, a spender must stop recklessly spending and instead consider investing if they want a wealthier life.

You should fear the possibility that, in ten years' time, it might be you who has less than £100 savings. What would you do then? And what will you do now to address that fear?

Emotional roller coaster

My aim is to disturb you into realising that you are probably heading in the wrong direction and need to make changes now. Reading this book tells me you want to be in control of your life rather than your lifestyle being in control of you. I know from my own experience that changing your attitude to work and adjusting to new ideas around wealth creation leads to a better future, but it is scary.

Making meaningful changes to your life always comes with broad and fluctuating emotions, whether this change is put upon you or created by your own actions. To help you adapt, allow me to point out seven emotions you will experience over time.[29] These can be used to predict and understand how your performance is likely to be affected by significant change:

1. **Astonishment.** Something in this book will astonish you and maybe resonate with you: perhaps the fact that 44% of the population have less than a month's wages in savings. Maybe you have never considered the working trap and didn't realise you may be in it. Astonishment will get your imagination moving and searching for new ideas. There will be a slight increase in your mood and motivation to change your ways.

2. **Denial.** When you have completed this book, you will probably recognise the issues I have written about. You will understand that to be wealthy you need to accumulate assets to some level, and that you need to work at developing yourself first and foremost, increasing your skills to generate the working income you need for the journey. The problem you will face is denial. It is easier to ignore that you have a problem and allow yourself excuses, to convince yourself that if you make a few minor changes to attitude or to routine, then major changes would not be necessary. You are in denial. Desire is not enough; you need courage to change.

3. **Anger.** Your mood drops further as you start to realise that you have been in denial. You will become angry and frustrated because if your desire to be wealthy and to enjoy your work is sincere then you have no choice but to make more significant changes. You have tried to avoid big changes and have probably made a few

improvements, but further analysis convinces you that these were not enough. The strange thing is, such anger is good. When angry your body releases epinephrine (adrenaline) and readies the body for flight or fight: run away or stay and fight. You are angry because you know you need to change and are about to do just that. You are in a state of readiness to change. The key is not to confuse this anger with regret at the change. There are circumstances when people half-change, to satisfy both the denial and the desire. This will make you angry and quickly you will revert to your previous position. On a typical entrepreneur's business journey they will probably experience anger and frustrations. Those who have succeeded tell tales of 'keeping going' because they knew they had chosen the right route to their dream and that change would hurt. Becoming wealthy is not easy, or we would all be wealthy. It takes effort. It takes perseverance.

4. **Despair.** Here, you are at your lowest point. You cannot be bothered and see only problems ahead. You want to stay as you are, fearing the hard work ahead, but you also know it is now impossible to revert to the old ways. Continuing on the new path is the only way out and it looks daunting. I have been there. We all have at some point but this time there is a difference. You know you are down and the next stage is upwards. Simply understanding the roller coaster of

emotions means you can see the future is good. Take courage from this message and keep going.

5. **Investigation.** The way to combat your anger and the fourth phase of the change curve is through exploration. You must commit to change fully if you are to see any benefits. Half-changes are of no use. Like the entrepreneur, commit to change, to personal development and keep going. Take comfort from a failed exploration: if it does not work, you can usually go back to where you started from, but commit to it fully without half-measures. Such exploration reveals new learning, new realisations which show up and overcome your initial denials.

6. **Decision.** Learning new ways improves understanding and invites more learning. The decision to continue starts to pay off. You feel more positive than ever and now see the old ways as laboured stagnation. You are no longer in denial, no longer angry and no longer experimenting with alternatives; you have made the decision to go for it.

7. **Integration.** Finally, after a period of effort, you will start to accept the new you. You will enjoy your work, see the benefits of your changes through increased income, and when you make that first investment into real assets for future passive income, you will feel wealth is now in reach. You will feel happier than ever and

this is the point of integration. Change is now permanent and the new normal.

The importance of your success may rely on your understanding of the emotional journey you will face. Please be aware, you are not alone on this emotional roller coaster. People go through these emotional changes every day; the key is to recognise what you are feeling when you feel it and why, which means you can control and understand the process. Following the mood swings of the work-to-wealth emotional roller coaster, you will find true meaning in your new lifestyle choices.

Life of credit – an opportunity cost

You have reached the time to either deny your need to change or start to consider that change is essential.

As I explained in Chapters 1 and 2, it is easy to drift into a life of credit reliance where you benefit from life's pleasures long before you have earned them. Allow me to astonish you further. According to The Money Charity, people in the UK owed £1,681 billion by the end of July 2020. This is higher than in July 2019 by £28.4 billion. Of this figure, credit card debt came to £62.3 billion, an average of £2,238 per household and £1,182 per adult. If you made the absolute minimum repayment per month, it would take 25 years and 5 months to repay this debt.[30]

Let me put this debt another way. On average, as of July 2020 the Citizens Advice Bureaux in England and Wales were dealing with 2,124 debt issues every day.[31] While it's nice to have the latest car, a new home and regular holidays and to regularly make quick online purchases of clothes, electronics and other consumables, none of these are assets that will produce an income for you in the future. Some are a 100% loss at the moment you buy them, because they are 100% consumable, like a holiday; there is no asset to sell on.

All this spending is the working trap that I warned you about in Chapter 1. If you genuinely want to be wealthy, this culture of benefit now and pay later must not only stop but be reversed. You must change to and adopt a lifestyle that is funded by passive income and not borrowed capital.

It is easy to remain in denial about this, as the change roller coaster shows. Allow me to move you further towards meaningful change by explaining how I did it.

MY TIMELINE – YOUR MOTIVATION

Age 17: I left school with a few O-Levels to work in my dad's business. I worked hard and earned but spent almost everything on fun. I slowly realised I was wasting time. For nine years I got on with life, the loves and losses, the fun and failures. I was simply living a life I had seen many do before me. As I moved into my mid-twenties, I now know I was in denial about my future direction.

Age 26: It finally dawned on me I needed to do something. I needed knowledge. I was the only asset in my possession, and I needed to learn, so I decided to get some further education. This meant leaving my work, leaving my hometown, selling my car and home to fund my new routine of study. My wife, my new-born son and I left everything and headed off in search of better work and ultimately wealth.

Age 31: After five gruelling years I graduated with an honours degree in Actuarial Mathematics and Statistics. This got me a good job with General Accident Life as a trainee financial adviser. Technically, I was overqualified but this would serve me well in the future.

Age 32: I moved again, family and all! Change to develop takes commitment and sometimes bravery, at times a gamble, but I spotted an opportunity to work for promotion and a senior financial adviser position soon followed, doubling my income.

Age 35: I won, on merit, financial adviser of the year and moved over to the corporate division, taking on more responsibility for larger business clients.

Age 39: I completed my advanced financial planning qualifications long before they were made compulsory. These included sales and supervision certificates, which pointed the way to future roles.

Age 40: I went self-employed and sought my own clients with a large national organisation. At the same time I started to invest in property, initially developing my own home with extensions and renovations.

Age 42: For the first time I was earning more to invest in regular investment schemes over and above my property development ventures. I continued to self-develop and to work in the financial services business, now training new advisers and becoming a regional business manager running a small team of recruiters and trainers.

Age 45: Courage led me to change direction again. I launched a new company called Truly Independent, specialising in supporting and promoting self-employed financial advisers UK-wide.

Age 50: I now had a thriving business, property other than my main residence and investments that I could call on to support projects. I continued to learn and grow all four assets. I bought my first Porsche: not unusual for a 50-year-old, but this was purchased with passive income.

Age 53: I launched my first book *The Happy Financial Adviser*, which became an Amazon #1 bestseller.

Age 57: I bought out my business partner, to own 98% of the company and be on target to achieve annual passive income of over £1 million.

From the point of denial at age 26, it has taken me over thirty years to achieve my goals and dreams. I did it because I backed myself, gave up everything I knew to better myself and to learn, and threw everything into the one true asset I had total control over, myself. You can do exactly the same.

Make more money – become indispensable

To put it simply, if you want to make more money you have to give more value and ultimately become indispensable.

For example, if you labour for a builder, you will most likely be on low wages and struggle with money. On the other hand, if you are the builder, you probably make upwards of £50,000 per annum. Over the year, you probably both work the same number of hours. It is clear to me that these two individuals are not really paid for their time. They are paid for the individual skills they provide and the value they give. Any builder can easily labour, but chaos would ensue if they changed roles even for a day.

To increase your income, you need to impress people more positively, to learn more, to gain more experience, to observe what others do and try to apply for higher-level roles. In truth, you get paid for the value you bring each day. Your income depends on how replaceable you are and, in sales, you are only as good as your last month.

If you hate your job, you could do what I did: take higher education for a greater chance of landing a higher-level job. Although I look back now and can see that my decision to return to education as a mature student paid off, I would have got where I am now if I had read this kind of book. It is not important to like your work, you must use it to springboard your route to wealth. You may not need a degree, but you do need to acquire new skills and your employer can provide those. Go ask them.

The more you learn and experience, the more you create a vacancy for yourself or secure a more important position in the company. Those who become indispensable to the company make more money.

It is possible to break away and start your own business. If you want this and want this course of action to be successful, it will be the learning and experience in your present employment that will earn you the right.

The employee – to change you don't have to change jobs

To help you increase your income, it is vital to change up a gear at work. If you want a better income as an employee, bring more value to the company. As an employee start by learning more about the company you work in, including other people's jobs and what they do.

Like me, you could study for higher education or professional qualifications. Ask for projects to give you more experience that will help your progress. It gets you noticed.

Read books on how the corporate world works and how others before you have risen to positions with more responsibility, income and freedom.

The entrepreneur – to change something for the better

This is a huge topic and there are plenty of books on entrepreneurship but be careful. I see the word 'entrepreneur' is often hijacked by just about anyone who is self-employed. The self-employed pay tax themselves and this is often the only difference between what they do and being employed, except maybe being their own boss. Employed electricians who go self-employed are not entrepreneurs until they take on staff and grow a business that runs without them.

The entrepreneur will generally change something for the better, to add value to the lives of others. They are the real creators. They build a business that delivers something to the market that attracts investors.

If you are thinking of self-employment, read about other successful entrepreneurs who have been evidently successful in your industry. You don't have to invent something completely new; copy things that have worked for others in the recent past and are still working right now, then improve them. If you are looking to build a business, bring more value to your customers and bring in more of them. If you do this, are willing to change, commit and seek to improve where others can benefit, you have the makings of a great business.

Key points

1. Don't be afraid to change your mind. In the words of Winston Churchill, 'those who never change their mind, never change anything'.[32]

2. Change is a positive search for better, for improvement needed to act on opportunities.

3. All changes invoke emotional responses: astonishment, denial, anger, despair, investigation, decision and integration (ADADIDI).

4. Avoid the drift and trappings of a life on credit, it's an opportunity cost.

5. To be genuinely wealthy, a life of benefit now and pay later must stop, be reversed and change to a life of accumulating assets and passive income.

6. It could take thirty years to go from work to wealth, so start now.

7. To earn more, you have to give more value and become indispensable to your employer and customers.

8. You don't have to change jobs, just change a gear and focus on what you can do to help the company.

9. Read more, learn more and take more responsibility; the money will follow.

10. Change has to be meaningful. Think of change as improving yourself, for yourself and for others.

Key message

Every New Year people commit to change something; but their commitment rarely lasts long. Change requires real commitment and will only last if you can imagine the ultimate outcome. If I can do it, you can do it; just follow your dreams and prepare for change. Unless you make the change, you will change nothing.

Key action

Change and the action of change should become habitual. Write down what small spending you can reduce or stop that will start the catalyst of saving, like giving up crisps. Make one change every week until making changes becomes second nature.

PART TWO

WEALTH

I have never been a fan of the words 'wealth' or 'wealthy'.

Deep down, it's probably why I am writing about wealth. It makes me uncomfortable. I know that if I do something that makes me feel uncomfortable, I am probably learning something from it. I am gaining new experiences, developing new cognitive connections in my brain and, as a result, new ideas can flow.

For some time now, I have observed that anyone who is wealthy is followed by the perception that a person's wealth is never deservedly earned (and often overestimated). I don't like the idea that 'wealthy' is opposite to 'poor'; it creates classes and separates people into them. This sentiment is the reason we named our investment house Truly Asset Management and not Truly Wealth, or Truly Wealth Management.

The moment you think about wealth, you think about the wealthy. Wealthy is a word that describes a person and their financial position. In contrast, 'asset' is a word that describes a thing; it does not extend to an individual (there is no 'assety' person). Wealth is the end product of some journey, for someone. What people hear or see of the wealthy often misses the risk they may have taken, the hard work, the effort and sacrifice they have put in. Wealth, itself, is subject to segmentation, privilege or even suspicion.

Worse, if you are wealthy, you are placed in a different group of people from workers. The title of this book, *Work to Wealth*, is my attempt to join the two stereotypical classes using an obvious and achievable connection. A person's wealth comes from a background of work. Sadly, few who work become wealthy, because they don't know how.

Do more with your income than spend, spend, spend

I have never wanted to be wealthy, but I have wanted to be self-sufficient and financially free without the need to rely on anyone. If that is what wealth means then, so be it, I am wealthy. I need to add that I do not subscribe to the idea that having your health, family and friends makes you wealthy. That is just a cop-out. I have family, I have friends and I have health (so far) but I can also add self-sufficiency and a want for nothing to the list. The idea that you don't need money as long as you are happy is a myth.

However, when we Google for current definitions of the word wealth, we get two nouns:

1. An abundance of valuable possessions or money.

    Example: 'he used his considerable wealth to bribe officials'.

2. A plentiful supply of a particular desirable thing.

    Example: 'the tables and maps contain a wealth of information'.[33]

It is interesting that the first definition is exactly what people perceive wealth to be about. Young people see celebrities displaying an abundant lifestyle and they want it too. They want money. However, I much prefer the other definition, the softer but more appealing 'a plentiful supply of a particular desirable thing'. A wealth of information, a wealth of money or, try this, a wealth of income-producing assets.

In Part Two, I will explain and define my version of wealth by comparing the passive millionaire to the traditional version. This definition links to the assets you need to be properly wealthy. You see, if you can live on £2,000 per week and are fulfilled, without the need to work, then in my eyes you are wealthy. You have managed to go from work to wealth. The only reason why you might desire more is because you have all the time to spend it!

I will start by showing you how to put a figure on your wealth by comparing an asset-rich millionaire to an income-wealthy individual. I will show you how three of the main asset classes – investment, business and property – will play a part in your journey to wealth and I will close with an overview of why you need help and who can help you throughout your journey. Enjoy!

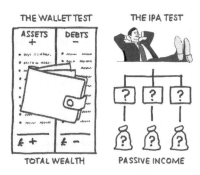

THE WALLET TEST

THE IPA TEST

ASSETS +

DEBTS −

TOTAL WEALTH

PASSIVE INCOME

6

Millionaire Measures

Two plasterers were plastering my lounge and I could hear them squabbling over money. They came through to ask me to settle a point. They asked: 'If the government has so much money, why don't they just distribute £1,000,000 to each person and solve poverty overnight?'

To them this made sense. I asked each what they would do with their respective £1,000,000; both fancied expensive sports cars. I then asked them what the sports car manufacturer would charge next week if all their stock was sold overnight? What would happen to the price of the holidays, luxury houses, flats in the city, expensive restaurants and nights out? Soon they realised that their £1,000,000 would buy little. Inflation would rise and their £1,000,000 would be back in the hands of the businesses that benefited from their spending spree. I pointed out that they would have made no provision for saving or investing any of their £1,000,000 gift and so they would be no wealthier than anyone else. Disappointed, they went back and finished the wall.

Being wealthy is achievable by everyone, and from a zero starting point too, but it must be about you and not about how your wealth relates to that of others. In this chapter I will assess the widespread, media-led view of what it is to be wealthy – boundless goods and luxuries – and my way, which defines wealth as something we can measure and target realistically, that can be used constructively.

Get rich quick

I cannot remember the exact age I was introduced to 'get rich quick' schemes; I must have been about 18 or 19. You sell a product and take a percentage of the price, or persuade the customer who buys from you to distribute your product to others and get a split of the price for no work. In effect, most of the business is generated through attracting distributors. I now recognise this specific business as a pyramid scheme. These schemes are not new and, while much business activity of this kind is heavily regulated or even banned in the UK, many countries allow multidistributor selling more or less unfettered.

Governments are wrong to do this. One multidistributor model may be fine, another may border on the criminal. 'Pyramid' schemes grow through the promise of fast wealth. Like the spread of COVID-19, one person infects many and those each infect many more, so sales grow quickly as tiers of buyers build up then collapse just as quickly once the market is saturated, delivery problems occur or the product is revealed to have 'problems'. Pyramid schemes rely on a pyramid of members to recruit more new members. Although there is usually some product to sell, a pyramid scheme is essentially a recruitment business. The schemes often fail when the supply of new members dries up. For example, if you recruit five people and each of them recruits a further five people to the scheme and this process continues, then it will not be long until everyone in your town is offered membership and the whole money-making idea stagnates. The people who start the 'pyramid' make a packet and everyone else is left with debts and bad feeling.

I think I was fascinated by the quick route to wealth. I now know there is no quick route and that even pyramid schemes, legal or otherwise, also involve hard work and time spent building distribution. Most people are sold (and then sell on) a concept rather than a great and certain plan to wealth: possible growth, not a practical means of achieving it.

There is a perception that wealth is only worth having if it happens fast and, if it requires time or effort, it's too difficult. I acknowledge that there is no quick or easy route to wealth that does not involve extreme luck, but there are routes that offer you some control and sustainable results.

Millionaire test

Who wants to be a millionaire? If you win £1 million, are you a millionaire?

The perceived way of calculating wealth is always by the sum of one's assets. Large house, second home, supercar, business, boat, shares and fine art (to name a few) are the assets we might normally associate with wealth. The problem is that a wealthy person can have all that and little passive income.

This person lives in their massive house so that produces no income. The second home is never rented and stays empty until they rock up at alternate weekends or school holidays as a 'getaway'. The car is leased through the business, the business only runs while the owner is present, the boat floats but rarely sails and the shares held have not been reviewed in years and could be producing little return. This person is asset-rich and cash-poor. They may have no debts, no mortgage and no liabilities but does this make them a millionaire?

I use two test calculations to determine who is indeed a millionaire:

1. *The wallet test*: Add up all the assets (or what they could be sold for, which is not the same thing) and take away all the outstanding debts, mortgages and other liabilities so what's left are the clothes on this person's back and what the resulting net assets are actually worth. Is this over £1 million?

2. *The IPA test*: Add up all the income this person receives without the need to work at all (ie as if they lost their job tomorrow) and multiply it by twenty-five, to see if that achieves £1 million.

Both these tests produce a single sum of money. The significant difference between the two outcomes is that the 'wallet' test includes everything, whether or not it generates an income, whereas the 'IPA' test focuses on just the assets that produce an income.

The idea that wealth is either an abundance of valuable possessions or a plentiful supply of desirable things fails to draw a line between where a high living standard stops and wealth starts. By definition, it is a poor measure. Such vagueness means we are left with only one way to assess whether we are wealthy or not and that is to compare our lot to others.

If someone appears to be wealthier than we are, it can lead to a chain of comparisons concluding in a feeling of underperformance and underachievement, and eventually the idea of being wealthy settles out of reach, so we give in.

Life-changing sum of money

Vivian Nicholson became famous when her husband Keith won £152,319 (the equivalent to approximately £3.5 million today) on the UK football pools in 1961 and she told the media she would 'spend, spend, spend'. Tabloid newspapers were filled with the Nicholsons' spending sprees and the money was gone within three years on a series of luxury holidays, new cars, clothes, household appliances and more.[34]

There is no doubt that Vivian Nicholson found it hard to cope with the psychological effects of the money her husband had won. Like many windfall winners, they had no idea how to manage or save money; they spent, spent, spent and ended up destroyed by their spending. Spending money this way has been likened to other consuming addictions such as gambling: spending becomes out of control and a distance builds up between you and the people you live among.

It appears to me that the public have forgotten this obvious lesson in the perils of windfalls, and probably many deliberately ignore the devastating facts about the consequences of such financial windfalls in the hope that all the evidence is wrong.

Alluring TV windfalls

If you have watched any daytime TV, especially the independent broadcasters, you will probably have seen 'cash give-away' competitions; and I use the word 'competitions' loosely. In fact, many have no questions to answer, but purely extract your data for entry into a prize draw with a small cost of entry. Typical prizes could be a new car worth £50,000 and a cash sum of £100,000. You would be invited to text a message to a given number and that is it. Of course, there is always the small print at the bottom of the screen telling you the cost of entry is £1.50 plus your normal phone charges, which could mean upwards of £2 to enter.

The prizes are always marketed as 'life-changing sums of money'. In one way that is true; they will change your life but they won't make you wealthy. Large sums of money will change your life, because you can now spend on things you did not plan to buy before and that spending will make you feel wealthy. It astonishes me that, when asked what they will spend the money on, many winners' first choice is a holiday. Never have I heard one winner say, 'I intend to invest the money and spend the income it produces.'

A £50,000 car and cash of £100,000 will do this for you:

- Replace the car you have with one that will cost you more to insure, to run, to service and to tax.

- The car will depreciate rapidly and eventually you will end up in a car similar to the one you had prior to the windfall.

- The 'life-changing sum of cash' will send you on a holiday that is more expensive than you would normally buy and perhaps you will take friends and family, too. Why not, it's not money you earned!

- When you get back home you will have £90,000 left which you will use to clear your mortgage.

So, you have a car you did not want, that will cost more of your income to run until you trade back down to what you can afford; the memory of a holiday that was fun while it lasted; and you still live in the same house, albeit you are no longer burdened with the monthly mortgage payments. You received a 'life-changing sum of money' but end up with a car and a home without debts. While you are better off by the 'wallet test', neither the car nor your home produce an income. As measured by the IPA test, you are in fact still £1 million from being a millionaire.

Keep this windfall example in mind while we explore the two tests in more detail.

Wallet test

I have a measure of my personal wealth going back to my youth, when I was just 17. I had saved up some money and spent nothing on myself. I owned little personally but was living at home and hence had little outgo to consider. I played golf with my dad's old set of clubs. I had just started to earn: my dad stuffed a few quid in my hand each week, having already adjusted for my keep. I asked for one thing only, an upgrade from my bicycle to a moped, which happened on my 17th birthday.

The moped, a 50cc Yamaha, gave me my first sense of freedom. It gave me speed, distance and a sense of maturity. It was a valuable possession. Freedom belonged to three of us: me, my moped and my wallet.

As time went by, the moped was changed for a car, a white Mini 1275 Clubman with black 1275 stripes on the doors and huge Cibie spotlights fixed to the front grill. I thought this Mini was wonderful and it made me feel happy, especially since it had only one speed: flat out! Like the moped before it, freedom belonged to three of us: me, my Mini and my wallet.

However, I noticed something. Although I had matured from a bike to a moped to a car, the sum in my wallet had not increased. To be clear, the money going into my wallet had increased but I was spending more on possessions and entertainment simply because the better vehicles provided me with means to do so, and cost more to run. Entertainment, by the way, provides 100% loss and yields only a memory.

Time went by, and the usual trappings of life emerged. By age 26, I was married with a baby, I lived in a new-ish home with a mortgage, I had credit card debts and, worst of all, I had developed few transferable skills. I was in the working trap! My retirement was also secured by a pension my dad's business arranged for us.

Familiar?

Don't get me wrong, life was good but it was a life mapped out by others. I had a pension before I knew what I was going to do in my 30s, let alone 40s or even 50s. My knowledge of money had leaped from working for a living to funding a pension from that living. I look back now and realise that not only was I in the working trap but I had taken the first steps towards the pension trap! It was clear I had to work for a living and that living might fund my retirement. I started to yearn for the days when all I had was a car and a wallet.

Probably over a glass of wine, Catherine and I started to consider this measure of wealth. If we sold everything, each left work and had nothing but us, our car and a wallet, how much would we have and what would we do? Just the thought was exciting!

We suggested to family and friends our idea to 'just go' and we were never taken seriously. So much so that we were dragged down to their way of thinking that such dreams would not amount to anything, just hot air. I don't think for one minute anyone believed we would sell up and go, but we did.

Those who know me today say I get stuff done. There is no time to wait and see, no time to ponder possibilities, no time to settle for the cards you are dealt. I say make haste and do whatever it is you want to do.

I still use the wallet test in my own finances. These days it is a spreadsheet that both shows the net value of my assets (while I live and after I die) and compares the wallet test to the better wealth measure of the IPA test. Below is an example of my spreadsheet, though the figures and data are just illustrations.

If this person were to sell everything and clear their debts then the 'wallet test' column tells them they would have £4,986,850 in their wallet. Anyone who won that amount on the lottery would say they were wealthy. Capital sums of this kind are easy to understand because we often see capital lump sums used to measure wealth. *The Times* rich list measures wealth in capital terms. But it's not realistic. The value would only be 'true' if you sold everything on the same day, and we all know some things are harder to sell than others. It is the income in the 'IPA test' column that is the true measure of wealth, because it measures the income you can count on, whatever happens.

Who	Assets	Asset Name	Net Assets (Wallet Test)		Passive Income (IPA Test)	
Joint	Property 1	House	£	650,000	£	–
Joint	Property 2	Flat (rental)	£	225,000	£	10,032
Joint	Property 3	Flat (rental)	£	220,000	£	8,131
Joint	Vehicle	Private Car	£	36,000	£	–
Joint	Banks	Current	£	50,000	£	250
Joint	Cash Held	Money	£	500	£	–
Joint	Lender 1	Mortgage (Property 1)	–£	460,000	£	–
Joint	Lender 2	Mortgage (Property 2)	–£	135,000	£	–
Joint	Lender 3	Mortgage (Property 3)	–£	135,000	£	–
Joint	Lender 3	Visa	–£	2,000	£	–
Person 1	Investment	Self Investment Pension	£	300,000	£	–
Person 1	Investment	Individual Savings Account (ISA)	£	80,000	£	3,200
Person 2	Investment	Self Investment Pension	£	–	£	–
Person 2	Investment	Individual Savings Account (ISA)	£	45,000	£	1,800

Cont.

Who	Assets	Asset Name	Net Assets (Wallet Test)	Passive Income (IPA Test)
Joint	Banks	Current (Alternative planning)	£ 10,200	£ –
Person 1	Paypal	eBay Account	£ 100	£ –
Person 1	bet365	Betting Account	£ 50	£ –
Person 1	Building Society	Cash Savings (used for Change deposits)	£ 2,000	£ –
Person 1	NS & I	Premium Bonds	£ 50,000	£ 600
Person 2	NS & I	Premium Bonds	£ 50,000	£ 600
Person 1	Business	100% Shareholding	£ 4,000,000	£ 196,000
		Total (Alive)	£ 4,986,850	£ 220,613
		Group Life (Business)	£ 100,000	
		Private Life and Critical Illness (joint)	£ 400,000	
		Other Life (Pension Plan)	£ 100,000	IPA Value:
		Totals (on death)	£ 5,586,850	£ 5,515,330

This person above has a passive income of £220,613 per annum. Be clear, this is income without working. Surely this person is wealthy! To produce a value we can compare to the wallet test, we multiply by twenty-five: £220,613 × 25 = £5,515,330.

The IPA test

The £220,613 gross passive income comes in from rent, bank interest, income from various investments and dividends from the company this person owns – in short, from property, investment and business assets. This person no longer has to work to earn this income. The IPA test says they would need £5.5 million in capital, invested at 4%, to produce the same income.

The key to maintaining real wealth is to spend only passive income and invest anything not spent. Money in the bank and investments are assets that have all come from passive income. There is no more need for earned income.

I strongly believe and advocate that the real measure of your wealth is not the wallet test (net asset value), as I once believed, but the IPA test. The landed gentry I mentioned in Part One were so wealthy, not because of the value of their estates and investments, but because these produced income without the gentry needing to work. Most of their capital was illiquid, as is mine, so money to spend ('liquidity') comes from cashflow.

Your overall aim is to accumulate assets over time by working at working and being the best in your game. This working income should be accumulated, first in investments, then in property and business, either as an employee or an employer. Your investments, property and business need to be structured in such a way that your income does not rely on you continuing to work – all passive income.

In summary, your desire for wealth must translate to a desire for passive income greater than what you can earn through your own efforts.

Cashflow

Turnover – the amount of money received by a business – provides a measure of the effectiveness of its sales and marketing. It's the money that flows into a company before expenses. The better the sales and marketing, the greater the turnover, sometimes referred to as 'revenue'.

By contrast, cashflow measures both what comes in and what goes out, and when these happen. This is a better measure of growth and of liquidity. Cashflow can be positive or negative, while turnover is always positive. If your expenses are less than your turnover you will have a positive cashflow, which indicates growth. If your expenses are more than your turnover, you will have a negative cashflow. Over a year, a company could have periods of positive and negative cashflow for reasons investors and managers need to understand. For example, a holiday caravan park will have positive cashflow in summer months and may have negative cashflow in winter months. So long as the year is positive overall, there will be growth, but the timing of negative cashflows can give cause for concern.

I remember advising a firm who exported grain from the UK on a group pension scheme. Farmers at that time (possibly still today) produced more grain than was immediately needed to ensure that, as a nation, we would always have a grain supply. It was probably a protective model after experiences in the two world wars. The company had a turnover of £52 million but its expenses were so high, the cashflow was only just positive, at £100,000 per annum. This company saw its purpose as ensuring UK farmers produced grain and hence it was exported at a low price. Neither efficiency nor profit was the force driving this company, it was the desire to ensure the population of the UK always had access to a steady flow of grain to remain self-sufficient, especially if war broke out again.

Like companies do, consider your working income. Think of it as turnover or revenue for your household. Of course, it's subject to tax, and you have to pay your own living expenses. If your living expenses are greater than the revenue, your cashflow is negative and that usually means debt accumulation. If your living expenses are less than your revenue then your cashflow is positive and that is the position to be in.

Let's say you are worth (by the wallet test) £1 million on paper. This could mean assets worth £10 million and £9 million of debts. Those debts are not an issue if you could afford the regular payments and living costs. Let's assume these payments and costs amount to £400,000 per annum against a revenue of £420,000 per annum, giving you a positive cashflow of £20,000 per annum. From this there are five points to note:

- The £10 million assets will grow.

- The £10 million assets produce £420,000 annual income.

- After paying £400,000 in costs and expenses, cashflow is £20,000 positive.

- The £9 million debts are not an issue since cashflow covers repayments.

- The £9 million debts are less than the £10 million assets.

Remember these five points and ask yourself five questions:

1. Do I have assets that will grow?

2. Do I have assets that produce regular income?

3. Is my cashflow positive (after all costs and expenses)?

4. Are my debt repayments met easily out of my regular income?

5. Are my total debts less than my total assets?

If you can answer yes to all five, you are on the right track to becoming wealthy.

If I am an asset, do I have a value?

The answer is yes. Your value is the cost of replacing you, or rather the income you bring in. If you earn £30,000 per year salary, then the cost of replacing you is twenty times your salary, which is £600,000. Put another way, it would require assets worth £600,000 and yielding 5% per annum to generate income of £30,000 a year. If you are thinking of life insurance, that's the formula for working out how much cover to buy, at least. If you expect to achieve just 4% income per annum, it will require assets worth £750,000.

In summary, millionaires are for TV, news articles and all media seeking to remind you of your poverty. Ignore them. Your wealth is what *you* need to achieve and is simply your dream best achieved by generating enough passive income to fund your chosen lifestyle without the need to work.

Key points

1. If the government gave us each £1 million, it would cause inflation and soon £1 million would be the price of the average car.

2. True wealth cannot be made fast, so avoid 'get rich quick' schemes, lotteries and competitions.

3. There is no quick or easy route to wealth, but there is a route that you could control.

4. Capital wealth is measured by 'the wallet test'. It's what you have left if you sell everything and clear all your debts.

5. Income wealth is the passive income you generate multiplied by twenty.

6. A 'life-changing sum of money' will only be enough if it can produce an income that replaces your current income: twenty times your income, or more.

7. The motivation to create wealth is only supported by having a purpose, a goal, a dream to achieve.

8. Household income should be treated like business revenue, with cashflow kept positive.

9. High debts are not an issue, if you have higher assets.

10. High expenses are not an issue if you have enough positive cashflow.

Key message

Don't get drawn into expecting a millionaire life-style and the celebrity world of luxuries and goods purveyed by media gossip. It's a false impression of what it is to be wealthy. You are wealthy if you have all the time to yourself that you would wish, without the need to work for a living and at a lifestyle of your choosing, that you can create and control.

Key action

Create the millionaire test spreadsheet as above on your own computer and apply the two wealth measures I have highlighted to see where you stand financially at present; then monitor this monthly for growth. Use these measures to set targets and goals.

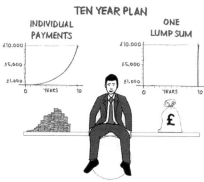

7

Powerful Investment

When I left university aged 31 with a degree in Actuarial Mathematics and Statistics, I immediately set about looking for work. As a mature student entering the graduate route to employment my age was against me and it also precluded the idea of a postgraduate degree: any funding for a postgraduate degree has a typical age limit of 25. Suddenly, I was broke – educated but broke. My wife was working as a nurse part-time and, other than a few holiday jobs, our income just about covered monthly expenses.

At this time, I turned to the state for help. They offered two options, unemployment benefit or income support. I applied for unemployment benefit but was told that, since I had just left full-time education, I was not entitled, despite the fact that I had worked for ten weeks in each year of education through the holidays at the local fruit and vegetable market. I pointed out that my wife had supported me, and had been paying her taxes and National Insurance. That did not count. I was then told that income support would provide for me instead, so I applied. But, irony of irony, this scheme considered all income to the house and that meant my wife's salary. As you will have worked out, we were entitled to no income support.

State support failed me, except for child support, which is available to every child in the UK. This was the last time I applied for any state aid. I realised that the first nine years of my working life, from 17 to 26, had counted for nothing. The state did not care about the tax and National Insurance contributions I had paid during those working years, and I had failed to accumulate any decent savings over that time. I was 31, well educated but broke, and entitled to no help from the state.

I vowed this would never happen to me again. I will work, invest, work more, invest more and work even harder again until I can draw on my own investments for support. The only thing you can totally rely upon is yourself.

The aim of this chapter therefore is to explain why you need to start investing now. Not tomorrow, but now. Getting started and regular investing for growth is the cornerstone of your whole wealth strategy. You cannot make money without first investing on a regular basis. Regular investment is extremely powerful and you don't need big sums to invest.

Consider this. Excluding the pence, over ten years at 5% annual growth a single investment of £10,000 becomes £16,289. A single investment of just £461 plus £100 per month over the same ten years at the same 5% growth rate returns the same £16,289. Increase the £100 to £200 and your investment grows to £31,807. While you might not have £10,000 just now, surely you can manage to invest £100 per month.

Once you realise this, investing is for everyone, affordable and therefore powerful.

Saving is not investing

I have a few important words about saving.

If I have two pieces of cake, eat one now and save the other for later, then by not touching that second piece of cake I have saved it from being eaten. It remains a piece of cake. I have saved myself the extra calories I probably don't need, and still have a piece of cake to eat later.

EXAMPLE: LET'S SWITCH CAKE FOR MONEY

I have £200. I spend £100 now and save the other £100 for later. By not touching that £100 I have saved it from being spent. I still have £100. I have saved myself from making extra purchases I probably don't need. This £100 will sit in my bank account, available to be spent later.

If saving a piece of cake is not eating it, then saving £100 is not spending it.

To reduce your calorie intake, you need to stop eating cake. To stop spending, you need to save.

Just to be absolutely clear, saving is the cure for spending; but it is not investing. If someone tells me they save £300 per month, they are actually saying they don't spend £300 per month. I want you to understand this mindset. Saving is the act of not spending; investing is a separate process. Get used to this way of thinking.

When you have stopped spending and learned to save money, you are preparing to invest that money. These days, virtually everyone receives salary or wages direct into their bank. If you don't spend it all, some will remain in the bank, but it's not invested and it will be earning you little or no interest while it sits there. Bank interest rates are almost always less than inflation, so inflation will eat away your savings' value. In terms of growth, it might as well be in a tin under the bed, with the cake!

Compounding and time

If you invest in a savings account in a bank or building society, be careful to ask how the interest is treated.

Simple interest is based on the amount originally deposited (the 'capital'). This means if you invest £10,000 at 3% interest, you will get paid £300 each year. Simple, yes? If you take £1,000 out in year 2, the interest will reduce to £270 [3% of (£10,000 – £1,000)].

Compound interest however is based on the current value of the investment. If you invest £10,000 at 3% interest (compounded) the interest will be added to the capital so, in year 2, the capital will be £10,300 and the interest earned that year will be £309. If you take £1,000 out in year 2, the interest will reduce to £279 [3% of (£10,000 + £300 – £1,000)].

The difference is best illustrated by a graph comparing the value of a single investment as it grows over time:

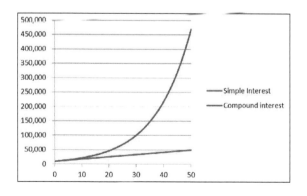

Simple and compound interest

Notice the effect time has on compound interest. Compounding is exponential in growth (curves upwards) and simple interest is a straight line.

If you invest in (buy) company shares, you benefit from growth on that shareholding and the profit that share generates (paid out as dividends). Most dividends are paid out as profit for each share you own, ie not compounded. However, if you invest in an investment fund that is designed to accumulate, the dividends are reinvested in the fund to buy more shares and the result is to compound your growth. Such funds are great for regular monthly investment over time and there are tax advantages if made through certain recognised investment products (eg ISAs).

Diversity and risk

All investments have a certain amount of risk. Even a simple savings account in a bank has some risks. If the bank failed you might lose your money, and because inflation is usually higher than bank interest, your money will drop in value. Banks do have some government guarantees against loss and in the 2008 global financial crisis the UK government bailed out several banks.

Risk is everywhere and has to be accepted but the level of risk can vary depending upon the type of investment you make. This is one reason why I would always advocate taking independent financial advice.

In general, if you are young enough and have time on your side to invest long-term, then you can take more risk than if you have little time and have short-term plans for your money. Risk and time go together.

Diversifying is how you mitigate risk, but it is not straightforward. If you have £1 on every horse in a ten-horse race, so long as at least one finishes you win some money even though you lose the stakes you invested in the other nine. To come out ahead, the winning horse will need to return you 10/1 (ie £10 winnings plus your £1 stake returned). Picking the outright winner is always going to be down partly to judgement and partly to luck, so backing one horse carries high risk; backing all the horses reduces risk but also reduces your overall return. Diversification is about finding a balance (perhaps backing three that all carry good odds).

The message for this book is not how to pick the best stocks (or even horses). It is realising that the amount you create to invest matters more than the return on your investments (of course, this is also important). If you give a financial adviser £10,000 to invest and expect him to return you £1 million in ten years' time then you are in dreamland. All long-term investment returns will be made up of both the amount invested and the growth on that investment, and the ratio between them will be not far from 50:50, depending on the growth achieved and how long the money remains invested. So if you want £1 million in twenty-five years' time, and you expect to achieve a return of 4% per annum, you should aim to invest £2,000 per month, which will mean saving £600,000 over those twenty-five years and gaining £400,000 investment growth.

OUR ONLINE INVESTMENT CALCULATOR

With an initial deposit of £0, monthly contributions of £2,000 and an assumed annual interest rate of **4%** for **25** years, your investment will build up to a total of £1,028,259.

A £100,000 investment in a fund portfolio can have the same diversification and growth opportunity as a £100 investment. If you invest on a regular basis, say monthly, each small regular investment will benefit from compounding on the others. Get used to this thinking and start investing monthly.

We teach Truly Independent advisers that a regular investment of £100 per month should be treated as a lump sum for investment purposes, so £100 × 12 months × 10 years = £12,000. Our advisers will give your £100 per month the same credibility as if you were investing £12,000 in a lump sum.

Here are my five rules for investing, which make the acronym ACTED:

- Pay for professional **A**dvice – it will pay off.

- Invest as much **C**apital as you can – it makes up most of the return.

- Invest early for the long term – **T**ime makes a difference.

- If you **E**xpect a high return, failure to achieve this will leave you short; if you plan for a cautious return, you might end up richer than you expect.

- **D**iversify – reduce risk through spreading investments or investment portfolios.

You cannot make savings without first generating a working income to save out of. Savings are part of your working income that you have conscientiously decided not to spend, at least not yet. Eventually, you will either spend your savings, invest them or waste them. Be conscious of these choices. To be clear, spending on essentials such as basic food, shelter and warmth should be expected and allowed for in your plans. Some spending is also investment, such as business training, buying educational books or attending seminars, since this is improving you, the main asset.

Investing requires expert advice

The financial industry likes jargon because 'experts' can charge to translate it. Having said that, most people don't have time to learn or understand a huge subject properly. So if you are short of time, hire an expert to help you get it right and get it done.

An accountant or solicitor can give some guidance on investing, but few have qualifications in investing and most are not registered with the investment regulatory bodies (so you won't be protected by those bodies). You need a specialist financial adviser and specifically an 'independent financial adviser' (IFA) who will be trained, registered, regulated and have access to every investment available in the UK. Strangely enough, IFA is also the acronym for 'income follows assets'!

Don't listen to your brother-in-law, or uncle know-all or your mate down the pub unless your brother-in-law is Grant Cardone, your uncle is Warren Buffett or your friend down the pub is an IFA. Keep your investing simple and start with an amount you can afford from your working income. If you can, after any pension contribution through your employer, aim to invest greater than £300 per month. The Office for National Statistics reported in April 2020 that the median annual pay in the UK was £31,461 or £2,621 per month, before tax.[35] If Mr/Ms Average adjusted their spending to ensure 20% (at least) went into regular investments, this would be £452 per month; if 20% after tax, National Insurance and pension contributions, £300 should be manageable.

I find it incredible that investing is not taught in schools, and therefore am not surprised that many save nothing. What everyone should do with their monthly or weekly income is set aside something for investment, *before they do anything else*. It's that simple. For example, if you take home £1,400 per month, you should first set aside at least £280 for investment. Then set your living standards no higher than the remaining 80%. Thereafter don't stick to the 20% rule, but try to keep living at that 80% × £1,400 = £1,120 and put every extra £1 from each salary rise into your regular investment plan. Don't be tempted to use your savings or the pay rises for anything else, even temporarily, because that's the way into the working trap.

By far the easiest and best way to simplify investing is to get someone to do that job for you. IFAs today are a far cry from the twentieth-century insurance salespeople. They are highly regulated and highly qualified to plan your finances for you and to control the risk associated with complex financial strategies.

You don't need to fully understand the jargon, but you do need a monetary target or goal to achieve and a date for achieving it.

'Many hands make light work'

This is an English proverb dating back to the 1300s. It initially appeared in a story called 'Sir Bevis of

Hampton' and has appeared in many proverbs since then. Most significantly, John Heywood included this proverb in his book of proverbs in the 1500s.[36]

It is a good example of metaphor, in which the words 'hands' and 'work' can mean many things. Investing is about using your existing money to grow and return more money back to you. This means that while you work, the money you earned recently is working too and making your progress to wealth a lot easier. Your assets should work all the time, even when you take holidays. They don't complain, but they can sometimes fail and therefore will always need to be managed. Experts do this for you.

Regular stock market trading hours in the USA are 9:30 am to 4 pm Monday to Friday with weekends and bank holidays closed. Stock markets in the UK open at 8:00 am and close at 4:30 pm. Strangely, there is a two-minute break at 12:00 noon. If you live and work in the UK, it could be your money works longer hours than you, at over 42 hours per week.

If you have not saved and have no investments, then only you are working, for yourself. By investing your savings you have created investment assets. These assets can return you a passive income and the more investment assets you hold, the greater the passive income you can receive – they are like a business partner also working with you. Fortunately, in the UK, much of this income can be tax-free, with the right investment plan. This is another reason why you need expert advice.

Set goals

There are plenty of books on the subject of goal setting so I am not going to go into detail here, but I will give you my simple view as to why everyone needs to set goals and hopefully this will inspire you to do so.

Football analogies work for me, and for my clients. The first thing is to understand that, when it comes to savings and investing, a goal is not the end point. Like in football, a goal may not win you the game, but without a goal you will win nothing.

Goals are short-term achievements. In football you can score three goals and still lose the game. Investing is about achieving lots of goals. I find the best investment goals are measured by the amount you invest regularly. Set your first goal at £100 per month, then your next to double this (£200 per month) and so on. Set smaller goals if you have to, but this will weaken your resolve and allow you to give in. You should at least save 20% of your income for investment.

Let's say you save £400 per month and invest it regularly. The next goal will be to manage to save £800 per month from your income. One month, you might invest £600 and spend £200 on your own education; this is still an investment. To achieve this you might need to assess your ability to generate the income. Remember, you and your investment work together. The goal requires you both to accumulate the investment and to increase your working income through promotion and career development.

Set targets

You have goals, so why do you need a target?

Goals are boxes for ticking and stepping-stones to the target. This is 'starting with the end in mind'. A Premiership football team may start the season with the target to win the Premiership league. To achieve this, it will need to accumulate around 100 points. To accumulate 100 points, this team could set goals to win at least thirty-two games, draw four and lose no more than two. If they lost three of their first ten games, their goals would need to change but their target could remain the same.

An investor who needs to generate a passive income of £30,000 in twenty years' time might set an investment target of £600,000. The goals to achieve this target might be to invest £1,300 per month and achieve a 6% annual return on that investment. All this is achievable and can be set up for the investor by a professional IFA.

The example below produces an interesting result that emphasises the importance of how time affects your money. Accumulating money in your bank for just one year (to build up an emergency fund, say), will cost you:

	Start immediately	Delay one year	Difference
Regular monthly investment	£1,300	£1,300	£15,600 less invested
Expected rate of return	6%	6%	None
Years investing	20	19	1
Asset accumulation	**£600,653**	£550,653	£50,000

By delaying just one year, you have accumulated £15,600 in your emergency fund, but after twenty years it has in fact cost you £34,400 (£50,000 – £15,600). It is not the first year of growth you have missed, it is the last year, and the benefit of compounding all the previous years.

I don't want to stop you enjoying yourself, life is about having fun; but I do want you to be aware of the implications of spending rather than saving. Just think before you buy. I am now able to spend and even waste money, because I have done the hard work building wealth so that the money I spend is passive income.

Set trophies

Let's assume your income is £30,000 per year from your active work. Your trophy could be to replace your income with £30,000 of passive income from savings. To achieve this, you will need to accumulate £600,000 as explained in Chapter 6. This is your target and you will set goals to ensure you generate the monthly investment to make this happen.

You therefore need to understand that, like the football team, your target is measured through goals and can win you a trophy:

	Trophy	Target	Goals
Manchester United	Premiership	Accumulate 100 points	Win thirty-two games
			Draw four games
You	Replace work with passive income	Accumulate £600,000	Invest £1,300 each month
			Achieve 6% annual growth

What you have now is a trophy to work towards. Something that fundamentally changes your daily life. To win the trophy you need to hit an investment target. To hit this target, you need to achieve smaller goals regularly.

To illustrate this further, let us consider something most people want: to own your own home. Imagine your dream property, its specific location, size, whatever your imagination requires. This is your trophy to win. The trophy will have a value: the price you must pay to buy this home. The value will be your target and you will also set a target date. All you need to do now is reverse-calculate the amount you need to save and invest. A calculator on our website can do this for you: https://trulyifa.co.uk/private-services/financial-calculator.

Of course, you might not need twenty years to build up the funds, because of mortgage lending, and so may only need to target a deposit of say 10% to 20% of the house price.

In this example, the house is the trophy, the deposit and a date are the target and the goals are the amount you need to generate from your working income to make it all happen. Notice, your dreams and desires all depend on your working income. So, don't go to work because you have to, go because you want to own your own home and work is where the money comes from for you to achieve this dream: your trophy.

Investment technology

Once you start investing on a regular basis you want to know just two things:

1. How much are my investments worth today?

2. Are my investments on track to achieve my target?

You need to know these two things so you can make subtle changes to your plan, if necessary. If you are falling short of your target, you may need to either increase your regular investment or add a lump sum.

Let's consider you have been invited to a golfing weekend. You know this will cost you £500 including travel, golf, accommodation and drinks and, if you play poorly, more in golf balls and friendly wagers. At this point most individuals will consult their bank account, or their credit card, but few would consider the progress of their investment plan. If you deprive your investment plan of £500, in twenty years you might miss your target by three times this amount, or more.

An investment strategy that is designed to be monitored using technology could help you to decide whether to go on that golfing trip, or stay at home and add to your investment instead. On the other hand, what if you checked out your plan and you were above target? That would be a fine time to reward your progress with a few days' golfing with friends.

Successful investing is about setting the right targets and being able to monitor progress to them around your life desires and your ability to earn more working income, until you no longer need to.

Key points

1. The state doesn't care about you, provides little for you and cannot be relied on.

2. The only thing you have control over is yourself.

3. Saving is not investing, it's simply not spending.

4. Don't listen to family and friends offering investment advice. They mean well, but seek independent financial advice.

5. Regularly invest an amount you can afford and set goals to increase it.

6. Many hands make light work. Consider your regular investment as working for you, working as you do, in partnership to grow your wealth.

7. Visualise the trophy you desire and, with your adviser, work backwards to find a target and set goals to achieve it.

8. Investment growth requires both time and money. The more time and the more money you can invest, the greater the return. Start today.

9. You need to know how much your investment is worth today and whether it is on track to achieve your target.

10. Use technology to track your investments and be prepared to top them up whenever necessary.

Key message

I could write about Individual Savings Accounts (ISA) or other savings schemes, but the rules change frequently and this book would be soon out of date. Investment is not about rules, taxes and details, it's about taking responsibility to invest as much as you can afford as early as you can manage, building as you go through life. It means taking action to put your money to work and letting professionals do the investing for you.

Key action

If you are unsure how to invest in stocks, shares or similar, then don't try to work it all out. Instead, seek independent financial advice and pay for it; it will be the best investment you will make. Refer to 'Your call to action' at the back of this book to find out how to find an IFA today.

8

Beautiful Property

I became familiar with property, builders and architects as a boy aged 8. My parents' business was growing well and like many business owners they decided to reward their efforts by investing. They chose to invest in a self-build home. There is nothing wrong with that since their business success was plain to see and their income at the time high enough to afford such a project.

The house they designed and built, with their architect, was beautiful, bold and modern, incorporating floor and ceiling heating systems. This was the early 1970s and I remember looking at all the designs their architect produced. It was probably the first time I truly wanted to be someone. People had always asked me 'What do you want to do when you grow up?', and up to that point I had always replied 'Play football for Manchester United'! However, when I saw the wonderful and varied designs of houses, I wanted to be an architect instead.

Our aims and ambitions change over time, and I never became an architect, but my interest in beautiful design never went away. I still appreciate architecture. In particular, I appreciate the difficult balance in designing new-build technology with the attraction of older and more traditional builds.

I suppose my initial interest in architecture inspired my interest in renovating property. In 1987 our first house cost us £30,000 for a modern, three-bedroom semidetached. It needed an upgrade, and when we sold just three years later we achieved £50,000 and a tidy profit. We used the growth to fund my five-year degree. I had at least recognised that I was the only asset I had and, while there were funds, I needed to invest in me if I were to progress. It was sensible not to plough the £20,000 gain into another home. Like those that win the lottery, we thought we had money, but we soon realised it was too little to achieve anything on its own. Although we had capitalised our property growth, I had saved nothing else.

The point is, had I never left to go to university, I would have saved no money and the growth in the property would not be accessible to us, because we would have invested it in another home and lived in that.

In this chapter, I aim to explain the basic difference between property ownership as a home and as an investment.

Your home is not an income-producing asset, yet!

This is your first lesson in property development. Your home is not an IPA and if you own a house and have a mortgage, then by paying off the mortgage you are turning money into a property that produces no rent because you live in it.

By all means, if you can save enough for a deposit to buy your first home with a mortgage then do so. It will grow and is therefore an asset, but not an IPA. However, if you can develop your home and increase the value, you are also increasing the potential rental value. The trick is not to use the equity to buy another home of higher value (the working trap), but to save enough to buy either:

- A new house for yourself, renting the existing house, or

- A buy-to-let, staying in your existing house.

Both amount to the same thing. You will have a house to live in and a house to rent.

I have done both with a combination of financial calculation and preference. In general, if you are happy to live in your present home, then so will a tenant be. In fact the best tenants we have ever had are those that moved into our old homes.

Let's say you buy a house to live in, hope to live there for five years and have plans to spend £20,000 on low-cost renovation, nothing major, maybe a new kitchen and decoration, new shed and boiler. Make sure that house is suitable for rent, not just for you as a home. Make sure it's a good build and you can see the growth potential over the next forty years. It's important that you like the house both to live in and for being attractive, practical and affordable for your future tenant.

Maybe, after a few years, you decide to move. The next house you buy is your own again. Don't make the mistake of using the equity from the first to spend on a bigger house with more bathrooms. Your new house needs to be a future rental, too.

A bigger house that requires renovation should cost you less to buy. If your existing house is immaculate after renovation and you rent it out, your next house should carry the same value and have the same potential. What you are doing is investing in growing potential by renovation.

So, if I have a house worth £300,000 and rent it out, it needs to bring in £995 per month rental, 4% of its value. If the next house you live in costs the same (£300,000) but after renovation could give you a 30% increase in value to £390,000, when you are ready to move on again your rental will be up to 30% more for the same 4% yield.

While it is possible to achieve rental income of 5% and 6% in some cases, the more likely income yield is 4%, especially if you use a property management company who charge for their services.

If you buy a house to live in, don't just live in it; consider it as a potential future IPA, following these three rules:

1. The property must be likely to grow in value over time so the location has to be good and in demand.

2. The property must increase in value with each renovation completed so look for high-value properties in the area.

3. The property must yield a good future rental so employment opportunities in the area must be good.

When you move on, you simply inform your lender that the property will be rented, take out landlord's insurance, place it in the hands of a property agent and wait for the passive income to come in. If you move five times in twenty years, you will accumulate four rental properties that effectively pay for themselves.

However you develop your property portfolio, it should be fun. I love developing property and, while at times it is hugely frustrating, it is rewarding and has become more of a hobby than a prescribed route to wealth – what do people say about enjoying what you do?

Property as a business

This is not for me and not something I would promote readily. It is also beyond the scope of this book.

Building a business from property investment, trading, buy-to-let and development is of course a route many choose, and they are successful at it. But don't think this is an easy route to wealth because it is not. Remember – there is no easy route to wealth. My personal route to wealth is driven by caution and assurance. Assets held are best spread. You are an asset, your investments in funds are an asset, your business is an asset and your property is an asset too. All four work together to create the landed gentry portfolio.

You are the main asset and, as you generate income, you invest it in stock exchange investments because they are easy to get into, especially if you take advice.

You develop your own business because you know about your product and the proceeds from that business should be spread into other assets, which of course include other businesses and property.

If your business is in property, and property values fall (remember the 2008 credit crunch) then so too does your business. The watchword here is diversification. I treat property investment as part of a mixed portfolio, like the great landowners. Land can be leased, property rented.

Property as a buy-to-let asset

If you never plan to move out of your first home, maybe buy-to-let is the route to property asset accumulation. Buying property for rental is a big purchase, but if you have accumulated a sum of money through your investments, some of it can be withdrawn as a 25% deposit and 75% of the purchase price raised through a buy-to-let mortgage. An independent mortgage or financial adviser will help you with this process.

In general, the property is purchased, and you hand control over to a professional property manager. Do not get involved in renting the property yourself, it's too time-consuming. Your skills are best used elsewhere.

Once rented, plan to keep the property indefinitely, repairing as the property demands. For example, tenants don't mind new windows going in since they see you improving their living standard and you improve the chance of growth in value. Slowly, over time, as you improve the property you increase the rental each year by small, measured amounts to maintain that 4% yield.

As you improve the property over time, the value will increase to a point that you can remortgage. Let's say you purchase at £200,000 with a £50,000 deposit raised from your hard-earned investments. After five years, the property is valued at £270,000 and you decide to remortgage at 75% again. This would be a new mortgage of £202,500 against the new valuation. The related deposit is the equity you hold in this property. The original mortgage of £150,000 is repaid and the lender sends you the difference, a cheque for £52,500. Note, this is all of your original deposit plus £2,500. You now own all the growth in the property, receive all the rental and have all your original investment back… and it's all tax-free!

The property value has increased by £70,000 which, if added to your original £50,000, means your equity has grown to £70,000 + £50,000 = £120,000.

	Value	Mortgage	Deposit/equity
Initial mortgage	£200,000	£150,000 (75%)	£50,000 (25%)
Remortgage	£270,000	£202,500 (75%)	£67,500 (25%)
Growth/ return/ increase	£ 70,000	£52,500 (75%)	£17,500 (25%)

You use this equity in a remortgage to release your original deposit back to you in cash and retain the rest in property as equity. While your mortgage has increased from £150,000 to £202,500, the equity you have in that new property value is now £67,500; and you have received £52,500 back to invest.

Understanding this – take a little time with a pen and paper playing about with your own figures to get your head around it if necessary – is an epiphany moment in property asset accumulation. Investing in property and the evolving tax benefits is not simple but it is beautiful.

By remortgaging, you release money to invest in another property, just as you did first time round. While this is not a fast way of accumulating wealth, don't be dragged into overborrowing to accumulate many properties, since you don't know the markets and what level of property growth you will achieve. There are still risks as many found out to their cost in the 2008 credit crunch.

Remember, property should be one of the asset classes you use to grow your wealth. I do not recommend it as the sole asset class; you must diversify. Buy well, buy good quality and do your research by speaking to property management experts before you buy to let.

Property and IPA wealth test

Overstretching your ownership of property carries risks and hassle.

Remember, the purpose is to accumulate IPAs; and property is probably the best of them. However, remember too your own target: to produce enough passive income to support your lifestyle so you don't have to work. Work out what property you need to passively cover your spending. It requires balance.

Let's say you set your passive income target at £60,000 per annum. If you are achieving 4% before tax from property rental, you will need properties with a combined value of £60,000 × 25 = £1.5 million.[37] If each property was valued at £250,000, then you would need six properties. If you reach that target then you have done well and could declare yourself to be wealthy.

The point is that you don't need a portfolio of thirty properties or a London apartment block to be wealthy. Set your own wealth measurement and go for it.

Beyond six properties, you are moving towards the realms of superwealth, which is of course possible; however, this book aims to make you wealthy.

If being a financial adviser has taught me anything, it is to control my risk, diversify where I can and avoid paying unnecessary tax. You are liable to tax if you buy or sell a second property, so investing in property should be long-term. For this reason, make sure you choose your properties well and only buy property you would happily live in.

Property is an illiquid asset. This could mean you need to have substantial equity in the property (at least 25%) and at least £200,000 in liquid investments (assets you could sell readily, if you needed to). While you might be tempted to buy more properties with that investment portfolio, I suggest aiming to have at least a full deposit for every property you already own. For example, if you own four properties and rent them out, and they each hold your deposit of £50,000, then you need at least 4 × £50,000 = £200,000 in liquid savings. Why? Because markets move, renters leave, mortgage interest rates change and, most of all, you sometimes need access to capital quickly. Let's say that blue moon property comes onto the market and a cash purchase, not a mortgage, would win the bid. Once bought with cash, you can remortgage later.

Property type

Most property gurus will tell you to avoid residential houses, semidetached or detached, and instead invest in apartment blocks. These are readily available in the USA but less common in the UK property market. Historically, in the UK individuals buy for personal use; a home is someone's castle, so to speak. Building apartment blocks to rent offers a slower return on the investment than building to sell. However, this market is changing as property prices stretch out of reach for many first-time buyers. In the UK the average age of a first-time buyer had reached 31 as at January 2021 and it is steadily rising at a rate of at least one year in age for every three years that pass.[38] This means that, by 2031, the average age could reach 35 – maybe even higher as the pandemic reduced house building virtually to a standstill.

There is absolutely nothing wrong with your first house to rent being the first house you buy when you move out to your second home. This allows you time to learn the process, the pros and cons, and is by far the easiest route to being a landlord. It is likely this will be a small semidetached house or an apartment/flat.

Alternatively, stay in your first home and invest in a buy-to-let. There is no problem with this being a small semidetached house in your town or city: easy to rent to families.

That said, you need to know where you intend to go with your property rental development. You need a route map.

Finding a property seam

When you have accumulated substantial investments and have by now one or two rented properties as well as receiving a small but positive passive income, you may want to set your sights higher on the property landlord ladder. You need to find property that is difficult to buy but easy to sell: typically a flat in a tidy block of flats that are in demand and well maintained by a property management company. These are usually found in city centres near large hospitals, universities or colleges, and with high-quality mobile employment, usually in the private sector, such as financial services. Tenants in these areas are usually well paid, in higher education or high-level training, so for them to buy property is not a long-term strategy. They live there to learn while they too accumulate some savings for an eventual property for themselves, probably elsewhere.

These properties take little cash to improve and command a great rental yield, in the region of 6% or 7%. Don't expect more than this rate; the average in the UK is 4%. Compare this to the average mortgage rate in the UK of 3.04%.[39]

If you find a flat like this, buy it and rent it because you have found a golden property seam. As these properties come on the market, you could buy with confidence unseen. This is a game changer, so long as you prepare to pay more than the asking value. Don't pitch at that price, but go in as a strong buyer at the lowest at 95% of the asking price for a quick cash sale. This is why you need £200,000 in cash, then sort the mortgage out after you've purchased.

To buy a flat or apartment in a high-quality block of flats in the environment I have described will cost you in the region of £200,000 for a one-bed, depending on the city you select, of course. However, the aim could be to hold five of these at least which would be property worth £1 million yielding £60,000 per year rental. Holding a 'seam' of properties like this benefits you in three ways:

1. You can take out a collective mortgage covering all of them.

2. You can take out collective insurance for all of them.

3. You can sell all of them to a single buyer for a premium, if you choose.

The next stage is to keep buying in that seam and, if you wish to be bolder, start another property seam in a different city. The principle of buying property and becoming a landlord, accumulating a passive income through buying and renting out property, is the same each time, you just repeat the process.

Property and mortgages

I don't claim to be a property expert, but I have accumulated a small portfolio of houses and flats that I rent, most with mortgages because, this way, the lender is buying the houses for me. You can do the same, but you need to accumulate investment money first from your working income.

Lenders will continue to lend to you providing you can show good credit and always put down a healthy deposit of 25%. Personally, I like a greater margin and my deposits are 35% these days. Your lender is your property partner. They lend to make money while you source and buy the properties to rent to make money. Both lender and buyer are supporting families and young individuals by providing properties they can rent while they try to raise enough money to buy. You are helping others while earning.

Be a good landlord and invest in the property. Ensure worn items are replaced early and before each tenant comes in, clean and refresh with paint where needed. Replace windows and carpets as necessary to freshen up the property. Why? Because it is your long-term investment and will give you a passive income for life, so long as it is attractive and easy to rent.

Key points

1. Your home is not an income-producing asset, because while you live in it you cannot rent it.

2. If you aim to clear the mortgage on your home, you are investing in an asset that can never return an income for you. To be clear, by doing this you are converting money to bricks.

3. A home, however, can be a potential IPA if you keep it and rent it out when you move to another home. This is the simplest way to accumulate property assets.

4. Buy property that is suitable for rental, in a location in demand with high employment, that needs renovation to increase its value.

5. For the purpose of diversification, don't make property your business.

6. Consider buy-to-let properties with a view to remortgaging after five years, to release your deposit while still owning the whole property and any rent.

7. Calculate the number of properties you need so that the rent replaces your working income, and avoid overleverage.

8. Search for a property seam in a suitable and desirable block of flats or apartments and prepare to pay above the asking price in order to buy into it.

9. Accumulate five or more properties of this type over time since a group of identical properties commands several benefits.

10. Consider a mortgage lender as your business partner, jointly providing property to tenants who need it; provide a service.

Key message

Investing in property should not be a business for you, it should be separate from your main source of income to ensure strong diversification. Property is needed by everyone and is therefore a great investment strategy for long-term passive income for you, for life. However, ensure you look after the property and your tenants with improvements, allow two months' rent each year for shortfalls and spend on improvements.

Key action

Take a close look at the house you live in currently. Would you rent it? Look at your area for properties to rent: are they attractive? Compare those to others in different cities and see whether you can identify a property seam to work towards. If you don't yet have a property, start investing your income now to accumulate your first deposit by setting goals. Learn about property before you buy. Remember, it should be fun.

START UP   MARKETING

WITH IT

MERGERS & AQUISITIONS

9

Aspiring Business Owners

I used to think I could build a business and, when that business was valuable enough and desirable enough to others, sell it. This is the model for many entrepreneurs: to build and sell. The ultimate end in mind for many business owners is selling their company, to get out at retirement.

There is a fundamental problem with this business strategy. Let's say a business produces an income for the owner of £100,000 per annum. This person lives a comfortable life and at retirement decides to get out and sell the company for £1 million. They will have to pay (currently 2021) 10% tax on that sale and will walk away with £900,000. This looks appealing on paper. Our businessperson has gone from owning a large, illiquid business asset to having £900,000 in hand. However, they now have no income.

Like many, this person does not want to spend the capital and would prefer to leave that asset to any children; so they can only invest and take the investment yield. If our now retired businessperson manages to get 4%, the income would be £36,000 per annum. A reduction of £64,000! By selling the business the person in our example has reduced their income by two-thirds.

By investing in property, they may get a better yield from rental, say 6%. This would provide a better income, but still lower than previous earnings and the capital would be illiquid again.

The message is, therefore, not to build to sell but instead to build a business as an asset to keep, because it generates a passive income. If it is run well and continues to develop and grow, the income it generates will also grow. However, regarding a business as an IPA only works if that income is passive and not dependent on the owner needing to work in the business.

In this chapter I will cover the main areas of focus for any aspiring business owner seeking to switch from employment to self-employment and ultimately owning a successful business providing passive income, and how to avoid the business traps that so many small businesses fall into. Then you will have a choice to sell or keep.

In a job or in business

As an employee you have a job, usually below a manager who gives you tasks, daily routine and, if the manager owns the business, pays you a working income.

Those who embark on the journey to self-employment think they are going into business. If you leave employment for self-employment, then you will no longer have a job, or a manager/boss, but you will own a job instead. Owning a job is not owning a business. Only when you hire employees and have a place of work that is not just your back bedroom can you consider honestly that you own a business. If you are unsure about that, see what happens when you go on holiday. If your income stops and your customers receive no service, then you are not in business. In truth, if you have to pause your business while on holiday, you are either employed or self-employed.

The self-employed route to wealth

The primary reason someone switches to self-employment is to have more control of their time, make more money and be wealthier. But be warned. Self-employment is not necessarily a better working model than employment. Evidence suggests that self-employed people generally earn more than employed people and work shorter hours, but the margins are minimal and not different enough to confirm that self-employment is a better route to wealth.

I do not see employment as a barrier to wealth and self-employment as the only route. Many wealthy individuals are employed; they just follow the same purposes as the self-employed and start by working in the right company. You don't have to start a company or own shares in one to be wealthy, but you could end up that way. Again, your route to wealth depends on what you do with your income and not necessarily how you earn it.

The reason to go self-employed should be to create your own opportunity and take responsibility for changing your way of life, from reacting to your employer's demands and controls, to more freedom to control your time for your own long-term financial reward. If you have worked hard and developed your knowledge, skills and experience, have invested well and own property to rent, then building a business is a natural fourth step in asset accumulation.

Building a business is highly rewarding but time-consuming, demanding and often stressful for little pay. Business builders do it to accumulate business assets that can produce an income without having to work much. It's about being self-sufficient and not just self-employed. (In fact, you don't have to build a business, you can buy one instead, but that's for another book.)

Ultimately, your aim is to build your business so you move from running it (director) to owning it (shareholder).

Business start-up

Most employed individuals in the UK earn between £25,000 and £45,000 a year, maybe with other benefits, company car, pension and four weeks' holiday per annum.[40] They manage to live on this income for years without financial hardship. This begs the question, that when an individual moves to self-employment why do they suddenly need (or expect) more money than they currently earn? After all, they have been satisfied with this level of income for years.

There is no doubt that the aim is to earn more money, but this objective should be exactly that, an aim and not an immediate expectation. Don't be drawn into anticipating high levels of income in your first years of self-employment. Building a business can take five to ten years of serious time and energy. You should first plan to create a sustainable level of income (profit) at a much lower level of revenue.

Sadly, too many individuals go self-employed only to revert to employment a short time later, usually damaged by the experience.

Don't be misguided. Starting a business definitely requires you to go self-employed first but be aware that staying self-employed is a lifestyle choice. If you want to be a business owner, then self-employment is only a transitional stage. I went self-employed in 2003 but it took me six more years to transition from running a one-person business to business development through staffing in search of self-sufficiency.

Step 1: Be self-sufficient

Self-employment should be viewed as a transition from employment to 100% self-sufficiency. This is your primary focus and the first measure of your future business success. It should be the first consideration and the first target you put into your business plan: a primary reason to leave employment.

Being self-sufficient means you are in control of your time, your own earning potential and hence your own destiny. Only when you have achieved self-sufficiency can you then build a strong passive business income.

Employment can be viewed as a life of dependence on others while self-employment may be seen as independence, but though you depend on nobody else you still have to work to earn. To build a business you need staff to take over some of your duties while you are active elsewhere.

Self-sufficiency is when elements of your income do not solely rely on your own time. To achieve this, you must ensure you employ staff to take on the work you have generated.

Equally, don't rely on new customers to drive revenue. Existing and repeat customers are the cornerstone of a successful business. The only way to achieve self-sufficiency is to be proactive in building a business that constantly attracts both new customers and regular repeat customers and having staff deal with them for you.

Step 2: Be proactive with your time

Plan your first few weeks in self-employment and contact as many people as you can to build your customer list. Everyone you know, and everyone you don't yet know, is a potential customer. It does not matter whether you are opening a coffee shop, an engineering workshop or some personal service, you need customers and this means you need to take them with you or know how to get them. Do your research.

Your valuable time should be spent on contacting everyone you know to explain the move you are making to build a business and how this move is beneficial to them. You are taking a major step and, as with any business venture, should be committed. Your current income and lifestyle will suddenly change. You will have more time than you ever expected, yet no salary. Put your time into your business. While you were employed, you would be expected to be at work for at least thirty-five hours per week. Imagine the contacts you could build if you focused on reaching people for thirty-five hours each week. Be proactive and not reactive. Find a customer base and contact them. Consider other methods of meeting people that do not involve others or any financial outlay. For example, join a local business society or consider presenting a topic at a local institute's event. These are all suitable and proactive ways of finding new customers. As a mentor of mine says, get attention!

Step 3: Manage your financial expectations

Lower your income expectations and save your money. You are building a business, so ensure you share your plan of activities with your family and ensure they understand that you will need to make financial sacrifices until you are fully self-sufficient. Your family should appreciate the involvement and support your transition.

Holidays have to stop. Unnecessary spending has to stop. Before you spend, ask yourself: 'Do I *need* this?' This may sound harsh, but you are embarking on a journey towards self-sufficiency, and any unnecessary spending at this time might jeopardise that journey. Expect to earn less than your employment income at first; you will reap the rewards later on. It is important to maintain an efficient business model that covers all aspects of business and not just a flat focus on base costs. Remember, while you are building a business you also need to accumulate investment assets.

Tax and status

Employment can be distinguished from self-employment simply by tax treatment. As an employee, you are subject to PAYE whereas a self-employed individual declares their tax annually. This can trip up many new business owners. HMRC is not interested in whether you can sustain a life of self-employment, they want your money. So don't spend money that you need to pay tax!

It is not self-employment you are seeking to achieve, it is sustainable self-sufficiency and it does not happen overnight. Success is not dependent upon your business partner, your new suit, your fancy office space or shop, or the car you drive. While these can all reflect status or activity, they can also suggest poor judgement to a potential customer who knows you are just starting your business; becoming self-sufficient will remain a direct correlation between the effort and sacrifices you make and how you interact with others.

Forget status, ego or your importance. You need to show you are in business. People do deals with people they like, know and trust, and so do staff.

On it, not in it

All being well, eventually you will run a solid, profitable business with returning customers. Chances are you will still play an active role in the everyday running of the business. You will have staff and you will manage them. It may be your business, but you have not created a passive income while you are still needed every day. The idea of taking three months' holiday is unthinkable.

In contrast, you have created a passive business asset if you reach this stage and can take three months away on a world tour without it suffering. Sole traders cannot do this. They have to work in the business to generate income. Without that work, there is no income. Their time at work is directly proportional to the money they generate.

I discovered the concept of working 'on the business' instead of working 'in the business' at an entrepreneur's event in London. It was a light-bulb moment. I had worked to build my business for over five years and struggled to find time for a decent holiday. For example, just three days into a week's holiday I would often get a phone message like this: 'Andrew, we have a serious problem. Can you give me a call as soon as you get this message?' I would also come back to problems and issues to resolve; how could I ever relax on holiday?

The problems were also never serious. They were always something that was easily resolved in minutes or that could be deferred until I came back. Initially I blamed my colleagues for being unable to solve simple problems. I did not know how to resolve this problem, until the light-bulb moment.

You see, I realised that I was to blame, because I had created a culture in which I was important to the business. I made all decisions, all initiatives went through me, all ideas were mine. I owned everything, so how could I think I could possibly get away from it all? Of course this meant I would be needed during my absence: it's obvious, now. I had to switch the business from depending on me to staff taking responsibility, and move myself to working *on* the business not *in* it.

Instead, I wanted to create new ideas only. This meant changing my working role and today I don't need to work at all. Daily tasks are all taken care of by the staff. Two directors make all the decisions and manage the issues. It is 100% a passive business. I earn well as a shareholder; essentially I own the business and do not run it.

Building a passive business

I left full-time employment at the age of 39 and went full-time self-employed, working from home. I was fortunate to be offered £22,000 as a redundancy package and took that money to fund my transition. I could easily have spent it, the same option that was available to me from the profit of my first house when we sold it.

The best thing you can do, as I did then, was invest this windfall in me. Self-employment was not a right to self-management, or some right to please myself, work less and be my own boss, but a route to self-sufficiency. I spent the next six years learning how to be self-employed and building a client list that would generate a stable income for years to come. At the same time I was earning, I was learning. I identified a couple of successful businesspeople; I chose to follow and observe some clients and associates. I simply asked myself the questions: 'how have they grown their business?', 'what do they do differently?' and 'what can I do differently?'

Without knowing it, two of these people under observation I now know were in fact mentors. Every business owner needs a mentor, someone you can learn from and adapt from. Everything we do and know is either absorbed by reading, observed or told to us.

I became an advanced qualified IFA and supported by a large national IFA firm. With them, I took the opportunity to recruit, mentor and train their new IFAs to the firm. This got me closer to the action. I learned even more about running a large, multiadviser business on a national basis. In 2010, their software became available and with it I co-founded Truly Independent Ltd. Today, it continues to flourish and provides me with a passive income from an income-producing (business) asset.

It is not easy but there are seven key stages in this:

1. Maximise your employer role first.

2. Go self-employed, and learn how to grow an income.

3. Take on staff, ensuring they are profitable too and benefit the business.

4. Give capable and motivated staff responsibility and opportunities for reward.

5. Build a team with an office manager.

6. Appoint a director and offer share options that will give ownership.

7. Withdraw from daily activities, retaining oversight only.

Getting the right staff and training them to your ideas is key to building a passive business. You have to start thinking like an investor/shareholder and not an employee/director.

I noticed the difference when I started to give each member of staff a defined role, which needed to be flexible as the company grew. We have regular weekly meetings to present issues and problems to me, rather than me presenting to the staff. I invited them to not only present a problem but suggest at least one solution. Over time, I find myself saying yes to most proposed solutions with maybe occasional input. These days, the staff solve just about every issue they come across. All they needed was reassurance.

Business for sale

It's not easy to find an accurate number of businesses for sale in the UK today. After researching various online aggregators, I estimate there to be more than 37,000. These businesses are for sale because the owners, who may have founded the business, need to sell in order to retire.

While these are good businesses, they generally rely too much on the owners to run them. Their retirement from the business would render the business worth less (and possibly worthless). These businesses always require an owner's input and the sale terms envisage the current owner exchanging future income, usually three to five years' worth, for capital today. The buyer of the business may have the same ideas for the business or different ones.

If you build a business that does not require you to work in it regularly, or even at all, then there would be no reason to sell it unless you needed the capital.

CASE STUDY: SELLING A GOOD BUSINESS

Kevin had a good business he bought and later sold. It was a property management company and looked after 250 properties for his clients. These properties were all rented and he took 10% from the rent to cover his business costs and provide a profit. In addition, his wife looked after the cleaning of those properties, which helped generate more revenue for the firm.

However, while the business generated a good living for the couple, they felt tired and struggled with motivation. Family pressures meant they had no choice but to sell the business. They felt that selling the business would relieve the stress, solve the demands on their time and provide some much-needed rest and a capital sum.

After crunching some numbers, they calculated a capital sum from the sale that would clear their debts and pay off their mortgage, and thus reduce the income they would need. Kevin could get a stress-free job while his wife could focus on other family demands. They also convinced themselves that property management work had limitations, with new law changes for UK property rental looming. So they sold.

There are three considerations missing from this thinking:

1. Firstly, the buyer of this business was in the same trade and clearly had the opposite view of the property market. This purchase increased his 350-property portfolio to 600.

2. Inflation eats into your money unless it is invested in real assets and can grow. Clearing your mortgage sounds a sensible plan, but you cannot earn from that investment in your main residence. While it's an asset, you will not benefit from growth in that asset's value until and unless you sell and downsize.

3. You have no income and therefore have to work unless the sale is a significantly huge payday, which this was not. In total Kevin probably cleared £500,000 but he still had to work – full circle.

Unless there is something significantly wrong with the business model, there is no reason to sell and every reason to build. They had missed the concept of transitioning from working 'in' the business to working 'on' it.

A better solution to their problems was to do what the buyer did and expand. With 600 properties, he would have more revenue to fund more staff to do all the 'in work' tasks for him. After a while, they could have outsourced all the cleaning for a low cost and grown the business to produce passive income. The new owner could also consolidate the two offices meaning, inevitably, some redundancies where roles were duplicated. In buying the business, this buyer doubled both the income and the overall value of their business.

You never get away from looking after your assets; but you can get away for a while. Rather than sell to the buyer as Kevin and his wife did, a merger could have retained the businesses while reducing expenses and easing pressure through shared directorships.

The aim of building a business asset should not be to sell in the future for spending capital. However, with planned mergers or acquisitions, an owner can still exit from business stress and gain a rewarding capital payday.

Business oversight

Let us assume you have reached the stage of self-sufficiency. You have a business, staff and the income you earn is good. Life is good. You could say with all confidence that you have a lifestyle business. Maybe you can choose the hours you work because you have staff. This is the case for most small to medium-sized businesses across the UK. But is it enough?

If you are a business owner, then you have an asset. If you have to work in that business every day, then your business is an active asset. On the other hand, if you don't need to work in the business and could take, say, three months' holiday without the business being affected, your business is passive.

I found the right individuals to take over my daily tasks. As a result, the business is growing faster and the staff are better remunerated than ever before. I have time to focus on other matters to help them grow the business, which I just oversee.

Developing as a shareholder of your business asset

If you have not worked it out yet, your business is only an asset if it generates an income for you, without your input. I am a shareholder first, I enjoy high-level control of the firm and I pay myself generous dividends. It is the best and biggest IPA I own and it is still growing. I can go on holiday, or focus on other adventures, knowing the business will not be affected by my absence. Think about it, if I had purchased shares in Tesco, they would not expect me to work in the company. Your business should be the same.

To summarise, you start out employed. You then switch to self-employment, intending to start a business. After a while, you have staff and repeat customers. Now you can transition from working in the business to working on it, by passing all your duties to others you hire. Eventually you have an overseer's role as the leading shareholder in the business. You can live comfortably on the passive income you have created from a fine business asset.

Mergers and acquisitions

As time goes by, and in my pursuit of greater knowledge and experience, I now know my next plan. I have built a passive business and refer to myself as a shareholder/investor rather than a CEO or managing director. I now work on identifying growth through business acquisition or mergers. In effect, I have moved from working *in* the business to working *on* the business and now shifting again, to working *with* the business. It's the next step to even greater wealth and I am looking forward to the challenge.

You need to know the stages and to take each step, one at a time. First learn to save, then invest to build cash and then invest in property, while building your business to the point it runs without you. Then you are ready to take the next journey, but before you do get yourself a financial adviser and/or a mentor.

Key points

1. Step 1: being self-employed is not the aim, it is the transition from employment to self-sufficiency.

2. Step 2: be proactive with your time, use it wisely, do not waste it.

3. Step 3: manage your financial expectations and use your money wisely; do not waste it.

4. Don't build your business planning to sell it; instead build a business to keep that generates a passive income.

5. If you can take three months off and return to a business undamaged by your absence, you have a passive business.

6. Focus on training staff to solve problems and not rely on you.

7. Staff who find a problem and need to approach you should be able to put forward a proposed solution to which you can say yes.

8. If your staff are capable, just work on assuring them.

9. Find, follow and observe successful businesspeople and use their experiences as mentorship. No need to reinvent the wheel.

10. Use your business value as a springboard to mergers and acquisitions in your industry – start to think like an investor.

Key message

As a new business owner or an experienced business owner, there is one thing you should take from this chapter that will make a huge difference to your ability to create wealth. Make sure you know and understand how you shift from working in the business (as every founding business owner does), to working on it.

Key action

Does the strategy for growing your business include recruiting people who can take responsibility from you and ultimately run the firm in its entirety? Find a person either in your company or externally who could be that person already or shortly, and who is not seeking to buy your business.

10
Independent Financial Advice

Hopefully, you have been motivated to change the way you think about your work and income in general, in particular the purpose for that income. Focusing on accumulating assets with your hard-earned income is paramount for your future wealth. Remember, instead of earning money to spend you need to think of your earned income as small monthly assets that should not be spent hastily.

Also, now that you know about assets and IPAs, you know that you need to put your money to good use and accumulate 'busy' assets. Assets are busy when they grow in value and produce a passive income for you while you do something else. Think of a busy asset as a business partner, working for you while you focus elsewhere. All you need to do is monitor progress; keep a watchful eye on your busy partner.

In this chapter, I will cover the different types of financial adviser in the UK, how their value is sometimes misjudged, and how to find the right independent financial adviser (IFA), engage their services, what to expect and how to prepare for a meeting.

Not all financial advisers are the same

The financial adviser you need should work with you, not for you. Seeking financial advice should not be a way to shed the burden of investment and pension planning, to 'pass the buck' so to speak. No, you should seek someone who will work with you, guide you, mentor you and help you understand what you need to do because, quite frankly, your future financial position depends on the action *you* take now, not just what an adviser can do for you. A financial adviser will make recommendations, but only after lengthy discussion of your needs and aims.

But how do you choose which financial adviser is best for you?

Regulated financial adviser firms are either restricted or independent. In other words, not all are truly independent. Clients can expect their financial adviser to have their clients' best interests in mind, but a restricted adviser can only offer some products and services, and some are more restricted than others. Unless you know the financial services industry, best avoid restricted advisers. That leaves you with an IFA. However, be warned here, too. Not all IFAs are truly independent of influential controls from product providers through funding, ownership, profit-sharing or corporate structure.

For many years, I have been involved in the recruitment, training and mentoring of IFAs UK-wide. My company was set up and developed 'with the client in mind'. Our business model continues to attract new advisers to join us every month. Our approach is to continually build the client relationship. Our advisers have an excellent understanding of the industry with focus on continuing self-development to keep up with the changing products available. They attend regular events in search of self-improvement and work on technological efficiencies to save office time and thus clients' money. The industry is highly regulated, and as such can impact on time and costs which are normally passed on to clients through higher fees. However, firms like us that embrace technology can keep client fees low. These days, use of technology extends to online video conferencing, digital signatures and providing the client with an app to view their investment. We provide all our clients with a secure web portal and an app access where they can value their investments, view their progress towards goals and add to their investments without the need to contact their advisers. Advanced technology like this saves valuable time for both the client and adviser.

Seeking advice means you don't have to make the investments yourself. You can instruct an IFA to make the arrangements for you. Before you head off to invest online, buy a property or grow a business, I recommend you seek the services of an IFA. It is the simplest and easiest way to get started. You can search for one of ours at www.trulyifa.co.uk.

Everyone should have an IFA

If you move house, maybe to a different town many miles away, you will undoubtedly register with your local doctor, just in case you fall ill. Maybe you are on regular prescriptions. Registering with a doctor in a location convenient for your home makes perfect sense. Why would you not have that assurance? After all, we are talking about your health.

It concerns me that when people are asked, they invariably say their greatest worry is either money or work. Of course, you know that working produces money, so you would expect these two to closely correlate. However, some way down that worry list is health. When someone moves to a new town, and seeks out that new medical practice to register with, why don't they also look for and register with a financial adviser?

Most people avoid seeking financial advice for six main reasons:

1. They see no obvious benefit.

2. The cost of advice and affordability.

3. The time involved.

4. Family and friends' past experiences.

5. The negative opinion of others.

6. Because financial advisers are salespeople.

I want to address these reasons in turn. In this book I've shown strong evidence that paying for financial advice will pay off in the long run. If you seek financial advice you should be on the right course to financial security.

1. They see no obvious benefit

Research from Royal London and the International Longevity Centre confirms that those who sought and received financial advice, and were prepared to pay fees for that advice, generally benefited over the following ten years. In fact, the data suggests that affluent people who take advice will see their investable assets grow by 24%, while the non-affluent (just getting by) will see an uplift of 35%.[41] Despite this evidence, 22% of customers have never sought financial advice because they don't consider it something they need.[42]

The fact is those who receive financial advice can testify to its worth, but quantifying the benefit has always been difficult. Those who take financial advice are more likely to invest in assets that offer greater returns, by gaining a better understanding of risk. Across the whole Royal London research sample, the positive effect of taking advice was to add 8% to the probability of investing in equities.[43]

The research also found that on average the pension pots of those taking ongoing advice over a period of time were 50% higher than the pots of those who only took initial advice. This demonstrates clear value in continuing advice.

Commenting on the research, Steve Webb, director of policy at Royal London, said:

> This research uses the latest statistical methods to identify a pure 'advice effect' and it is strikingly large. If financial advice can add upwards of £40,000 to your wealth over a decade compared with not taking advice, it is incumbent on government, regulators, providers and the advice profession to work together to make sure that more people are sharing in this uplift.[44]

2. The cost of advice and affordability

This is by far the biggest barrier to advice. Royal London found that despite 47% of non-advised customers believing that professional financial advice will cost too much, most do not know what a financial adviser might charge.

Driven by myths and misconceptions there remains lots of customer confusion around what advisers do and the value they add. Royal London found that over 44% believe advisers are only interested in selling them something. Could this be the same 44% that have less than a month's wages in savings?[45] Yet the general public buy things they don't need all the time and, when it comes to something everyone needs (financial advice), take-up is limited.

The Financial Conduct Authority works on the idea that no one wants to pay for financial advice and continually seeks new non-advised ways to inform the general public, and help them make their own financial decisions. Even so, about 15,000 financial advisers operate in the UK today and they're all busy.

There are two real reasons why many people do not want to pay for advice:

1. They are not used to doing so. Until 2013 most advisers' earnings came from commissions on the products they promoted.

2. Advice appears expensive. A 3% charge on an investment of £100,000 would be £3,000. If you don't really know what you're paying for, so you can't make meaningful comparisons with what other professions charge, this appears high.

In a document published by Royal London in April 2021, 'Exploring the advice gap', they state that 'on average, professional financial advice leads to people being £47k better off after 10 years' and 'simply talking to a financial adviser helps people feel more in control of their money, confident about the future and better prepared to deal with life's shocks'. If the advice had cost you less than a tenth of this, being £47,000 better off after ten years would be good value.[46]

Further, Royal London claims that 'despite these significant benefits, only 26% of the country seek professional financial advice'. This means almost 74% of the UK population miss out on the true value of financial advice: the alleviation of financial worries it can provide. It is estimated that 39 million adults in the UK don't take any form of professional advice or guidance when it comes to their finances. This is the 'advice gap' Royal London are referring to.

Mark Twain once wrote: 'All you need in this life is ignorance and confidence; then success is sure',[47] but confidence and ignorance around investing can be devastating.

3. The time involved

The time it takes to meet and discuss their own financial position can put people off. Many feel their finances are too simple to warrant an adviser spending any time with them. The image is that advisers are only interested in customers wealthier than they are.

Money takes time to earn, so you should take time to ensure it is invested wisely from the outset. Of course, financial advisers do seek and advise wealthy clients. Any financial adviser worth their salt is going to spend time with you asking important questions to engage with both your financial position and your ambitions. Some questions will drill down hard into your thoughts and open matters you have not considered. Taking time now could save you time in the future. Why work longer than you need to? Unless of course you absolutely love working.

You don't need to prepare much but do have all your financial papers and statements to hand. Be prepared to answer questions honestly and truthfully. You will be asked questions that fall into a variety of categories:

- Your objectives
- Your income and outgo
- Your assets and liabilities
- Your plans for retirement

- Your education
- Your investment experiences (for experienced investors, the style you prefer)
- Your health, and short-, medium- and long-term plans
- Your attitude to risk

It may be your advisers will go deeper and ask questions about:

- Your experiences with money, success or failure
- Your general attitude to money
- Your purpose and goals
- Your family relationships, good, bad and indifferent
- Your experiences growing up, parents and family experiences

These questions all take time to answer and your answers will help your financial advisers to gain a true picture of your overall financial position now, the hard facts, but also the more important opinions, ambitions and goals.

Meeting with an experienced IFA will release financial pressure and be an experience you probably did not expect. It's financial therapy and worth every minute. The initial consultation is usually provided at no charge.

4. Family and friends' past experiences

One of the best questions an adviser can ask their client is to explain their parents' experience of financial advisers. It may be that their experience influenced your views.

People are private, especially in the UK, and talking about their money with a stranger is uncomfortable for some. The Royal London report I mentioned above found that 17% of non-advised customers are either too proud or too embarrassed to talk to someone about how to manage their finances. More positively, 32% of all non-advised customers say they would find financial advice more appealing if they could do everything digitally.

Many people assume friends and family know more than they actually do. These conversations with friends and family will often bring an unreliable opinion or be so negative that you do nothing. When was the last time you asked a friend or family member for some advice and they replied, 'Don't ask me; I haven't a clue; I recommend you ask a professional'?

The truth is, you need clear, expert advice when your aim is to grow assets.

5. The negative opinion of others

You may have found that those who don't know what you do still have an opinion about it, and that some who think they know, actually don't.

The Royal London report I have cited many times in this chapter found that 29% of non-advised customers feel they can't trust an adviser – or don't know how to find a good one – while 27% would be likely to see an adviser once prompted with better information about the services advisers offer.

Today's advisers are a far cry from the insurance sales-people of the past. In 1990 there were about 220,000 'independent insurance brokers' and today about 15,000 IFAs are in practice, maybe even fewer. Why? Because of high regulation, exams and the need for continuing professional development.

I believe, however, that the negative stories you may hear are born from our government too, in particular the Financial Conduct Authority (FCA), the regulator which oversees both financial advice and financial products. It is now over 25 years since the regulatory regime was introduced and, during that time, the chief policy maker has been the FCA (Financial Services Authority prior to 2013). By law, these regulators are accountable only to the Treasury Select Committee and they have no commercial liability for any of their actions.

The regulator believes that, with the right information, consumers can make their own financial decisions. In turn, this tends to reinforce the idea that financial advice is not required. The problem is that since 46% of young people (aged 16 to 24) don't read in their spare time and since, as specifically reported in England, as many as 31% don't read at all, their information comes from family, friends, the pub, social media and media commentary.[48] This calls the FCA assumption into question, though some might put it more strongly.

I disagree with them. I think there is a clear need for financial advisers and undermining them is playing into the hands of rogues and con men. I suggest you ignore the state. They are ignoring real evidence. Do not attempt to invest yourself, especially if you want success. Take advice from a professional IFA and happily pay for their expertise.

6. Financial advisers are salespeople

Most financial advisers today have come from an industry that started in product sales and that background is hard to erase; it's natural to sell a product.

This leads to consumers ignoring financial advisers and looking after their own money. Royal London again reports that 35% of non-advised customers think advisers can't offer them anything that they can't take care of themselves. This compares with previous research which has shown advised customers not only feel more informed about financial matters, they are also financially better off.[49]

Advisers want to make a positive difference in people's lives. They are highly qualified, regularly assessed and heavily regulated. As I mentioned in 5. above, today there are fewer than 10% of the number there used to be, thirty years ago. All regulated investment advisers nowadays provide advice for fees, not products for commission, and the industry solves many clients' financial issues with FCA-regulated financial products.

Just to emphasise how small the number of financial advisers is, according to the Central Council of Accounting Bodies (CCAB) there are around 275,000 accountants within the UK and Ireland.[50]

Aims, goals and ambitions

Targeting outcomes and setting goals are essential to achieving wealth, and an IFA will identify what problems you have and focus on the best route to address those problems. They will help you set financial goals and targets to achieve and provide you with the technology to monitor your progress yourself while observing your progress from behind the schemes, guiding your every step.

What people don't appreciate, is that there are two main problems, each with a host of sub-problems underneath:

- Not enough assets to do what you want (Insufficiency), or

- More assets than needed (Oversufficiency).

Only when the main problem is established can a solution be discussed. The Insufficient need to invest, the Oversufficient need to gift (if they want to preserve their wealth). Remembering this simple distinction will help you find solutions and gain the help and advice you need.

Engaging with a highly trained, regulated IFA will allow you to start your plan from work to wealth and gain a mentor to guide you on your journey. If you fall into the 'insufficient' category your adviser will suggest clear and achievable goals and targets to move you out of it. If you are in the 'oversufficient' category (wealthy) your adviser will help you to ensure both that you retain that position and, by making a plan to pass your wealth on, that you control the tax your beneficiaries have to pay in inheriting your assets.

Work to wealth does not stop. If you are not working to build your assets, you must work to retain them. If you build a business of any kind, it is normal to employ someone to work with you in that business and/or to hire experts to take on various roles. You will equally need someone to help you to fully understand the need to gift and how to plan for it. It's about understanding the big picture. How you invest or how you gift is where the advice process starts. That's where you need high-quality and truly independent financial advice; most people have to (or choose to) buy in these skills.

In summary, I'd offer a word to the wise: take advice; and a word to the foolish: take heed.

Key points

1. Seeking independent financial advice from a regulated adviser is a wise move.

2. An adviser is there to guide and encourage you on matters you probably have not considered or did not know.

3. Be prepared to provide information and answer drilling questions.

4. Everyone should have an IFA just as they have a doctor.

5. An adviser can uplift your wealth as much as 35%.

6. The cost of advice is much less than the uplift over a typical ten-year period.

7. It takes time to earn, so take time to take advice.

8. Unless they are financial advisers, ignore financial advice from family and friends.

9. The state will not look after you.

10. Financial advice in the UK has been regulated by the FCA since 2013.

Key message

I am pretty sure you have a doctor you visit when you are ill. If you run a business, you will have an accountant and, if you have made a will, you have probably used a solicitor. Since the biggest single thing you work for is money, then you equally need a financial adviser. A good one is worth the money.

Key action

Go to www.trulyifa.co.uk and, by entering your post-code, search for one of our IFAs near you. Call them and arrange a no-obligations meeting. Most advisers do not charge for your first meeting, so you have nothing but time to lose and everything to gain.

Final Thoughts

You don't have to be wealthy; you don't have to like your work. It is your life.

Having built a business, I recognise that my own pursuit of personal wealth inevitably impacts on others. We employ over 80 advisers and staff, there are more than 200 product providers with whom we have agencies, various business partners and associates we use, and last but not least more than 12,000 clients with over £1.3 billion in assets under management, as at November 2021. Our business touches many people and all benefit from each other. By working hard and building a business I have helped to generate wealth elsewhere.

This book is my attempt to contact other people currently outside our business: to offer the wisdom of my experiences and hopefully to influence you with the same enthusiasm I have generated for myself. When you start your journey, it will take effort and commitment, but soon you will generate your own momentum. In the end, it is not just you that benefits, it is everyone you influence. The satisfaction I get in seeing employees flourish and enjoy their work is rewarding, and is equal to the financial benefits. In making yourself wealthy, you are indirectly making others wealthy too. That's why you *must* act on my message. Don't work because you have to, work because you want to and make sure your income makes you truly wealthy.

Your Call To Action

When I read a book, I find about 10% sticks in the memory straight away and 90% is understood but requires a refresh. I recommend that you read the book again and this time, make notes on a separate page. Those notes should translate into a set of action points for you to focus on.

However, assuming you won't take notes, I placed a set of key points, key messages and key actions at the end of each chapter. Your call to action is to at least write down this set of key learning points, identify those that resonate with you and act on them.

Investing – how do I get started?

Good question. Investing your income is the most important step, and the first one to attaining wealth. You need to benefit from time, so start today.

Do not hesitate: go to www.trulyifa.co.uk and enter your postcode.

The results will show you one of our Truly Independent financial advisers near to you. Follow the instructions and make contact with them. Tell them you have read this book and are looking for their advice. You don't need to do anything else; they will take it from there.

I wish you wealth and happiness, though not necessarily in that order!

Notes

1 'Social Mobility Pledge', available at www.socialmobilitypledge.org (accessed 3 November 2021).

2 Johann Wolfgang von Goethe, *Faust*, Part One, 1835 translation by John Anster.

3 No firm source can be found. In 1962 *Forbes* magazine printed a version of the adage in a section called 'Thoughts on the business of life', credited to Edison.

4 Olive Pometsey and David Taylor, 'Average UK salary: ever wondered how you stack up?', *GQ*, 18 January 2022, www.gq-magazine.co.uk/article/average-uk-salary (accessed 8 February 2022).

5 D Clark, 'Number of people employed in the United Kingdom from March 1971 to August

2021', Statista.com, 12 October 2021, available at www.statista.com/statistics/281998/employment-figures-in-the-united-kingdom-uk (accessed 10 November 2021).

6   'Global wealth databook 2021', Credit Suisse Research Institute, June 2021, available at www.credit-suisse.com/media/assets/corporate/docs/about-us/research/publications/global-wealth-databook-2021.pdf (accessed 8 February 2022).

7   Robert Joyce, Thomas Pope and Barra Roantree, 'The characteristics and incomes of the top 1%', Institute for Fiscal Studies, IFS Briefing Note BN254, available at https://ifs.org.uk/uploads/BN254-Characteristics-and-Incomes-Of-The-Top-1%25.pdf (accessed 11 November 2021).

8   'Average weekly earnings in Great Britain: January 2022', ONS, 18 January 2022, available at www.ons.gov.uk/employmentandlabourmarket/peopleinwork/employmentandemployeetypes/bulletins/averageweeklyearningsingreatbritain/january2022 (accessed 8 February 2022).

9   Joyce, Pope and Roantree, 'The top 1%'.

10 Andrew Goodwin, *The Happy Financial Adviser: How to connect with more clients, enjoy more freedom and make a positive difference* (Rethink Press, 2017).

11 Janet Berry-Johnson, 'Income', Investopedia, 7 September 2021, available at www.investopedia.com/terms/i/income.asp (accessed 11 November 2021).

12 Adam Barone, 'What is an asset?', Investopedia, 28 February 2021, available at www. investopedia.com/terms/a/asset.asp (accessed 11 November 2021).

13 HSBC, '8.5 million UK households would not last the week on their savings', HSBC News Release, 21 December 2014, available at www. about.hsbc.co.uk/-/media/uk/en/news-and-media/rbwm/150310-savings-cushion?la=en-gb (accessed 11 November 2021).

14 Andy Webb, 'Millions at risk with savings of £100 or less', Moneyhelper.org.uk, 26 September 2016, available at https://blog.moneyhelper.org. uk/blog/millions-at-risk-with-savings-of-100-or-less (accessed 11 November 2021).

15 Lottoland, 'People behind the game – lottery demographics', by Nigel, 6 April 2018, available at www.lottoland.co.uk/magazine/lottery-demographics.html (accessed 11 November 2021).

16 Matthew Smith, 'How many Brits like their jobs and their wages?', YouGov.co.uk, 3 August 2017, available at https://yougov.co.uk/topics/politics/articles-reports/2017/08/03/love-wage-balance-how-many-brits-their-job-and-the (accessed 12 November 2021).

17 Smith, 'How many Brits like their jobs?'

18 Robert Half Executive Search, 'Route to the top: MBAs and accountants lead the FTSE 100', 11 July 2019, available at www.roberthalf.co.uk/press/route-top-mbas-and-accountants-lead-ftse-100 (accessed 1 November 2021).

19 'About Grant Cardone', Amazon (undated), available at www.amazon.co.uk/Grant-Cardone/e/B0038X6X5W/ref=aufs_dp_mata_dsk (accessed 12 November 2021).

20 'Amazon's stock to rise as growth continues', *Forbes*, Trefis Team Contributor & Great Speculations Contributor Group, 13 August 2021, available at www.forbes.com/sites/greatspeculations/2021/08/13/amazons-stock-to-rise-as-growth-continues/?sh=692cdfbe4788 (accessed 12 November 2021).

21 The Money Charity, 'Money Statistics, May 2021', The Money Charity, Archives, available at https://themoneycharity.org.uk/money-statistics/may-2021 (accessed 12 November 2021).

22 Wikipedia, 'Landed gentry', Wikipedia.org, 29 October 2021, available at https://en.wikipedia.org/wiki/Landed_gentry (accessed 1 November 2021).

23 Scott Nelson, 'Average mortgage debt – complete overview, analysis with FAQs & more', moneynerd, 1 February 2022, available at https://moneynerd.co.uk/average-mortgage-debt (accessed 8 February 2022).

24 Daniel Priestley, *Key Person of Influence*, 3rd edition (Rethink Press, 2014).

25 Joyce, Pope and Roantree, 'The top 1%'.

26 HSBC, '8.5 million UK households would not last the week'.

27 Wikipedia, 'Spanish flu', Wikipedia.org, 23 October 2021, available at https://

en.wikipedia.org/wiki/Spanish_flu (accessed 19 January 2022).

28 Wikipedia, 'Roaring Twenties', Wikipedia. org, 18 January 2022, available at https://en.wikipedia.org/wiki/Roaring_Twenties (accessed 19 January 2022).

29 This is based on Elizabeth Kübler-Ross's Change Curve®. For more details, see www.ekrfoundation.org/5-stages-of-grief/change-curve (accessed 3 January 2022).

30 The Money Charity, 'Money Statistics, September 2020', The Money Charity, Archives, available at https://themoneycharity.org.uk/money-statistics/september-2020 (accessed 3 January 2022).

31 Money Charity, 'Money Statistics, September 2020'.

32 Churchill adapted this from George Bernard Shaw – 'those who cannot change their minds cannot change anything', *Everybody's Political What's What*, 1944.

33 'Wealth', Lexico online dictionary, available at www.lexico.com/definition/wealth (accessed 8 February 2022).

34 Caroline Davies, '"Spend, spend, spend" football pools winner, Viv Nicholson, dies aged 79', *Guardian*, 12 April 2015, available at www.theguardian.com/theobserver/2003/jul/06/features.magazine67 (accessed 12 November 2021).

35 Reported in Olive Pometsey and David Taylor, 'Average UK salary: ever wondered how you stack up?', *GQ*, 18 January 2022, available at www.gq-magazine.co.uk/article/average-uk-salary (accessed 11 August 2021).

36 'Many hands make light work meaning', Writing Explained, no date, available at https://writingexplained.org/idiom-dictionary/many-hands-make-light-work (accessed 8 February 2022).

37 The IPA test (see Chapter 6) used a multiplier of twenty, because the expected return was 5%; here, we are expecting a 4% return, so the multiplier is twenty-five.

38 Helen Crane, 'Rising house prices and a mortgage crunch push average first-time buyer deposits up £11,000 to £57,000…', ThisIsMoney.co.uk, 25 January 2021, available at www.thisismoney.co.uk/money/mortgageshome/article-9177085/Will-2021-end-time-buyer-squeeze-sent-deposits-57k.html (accessed 8 February 2022).

39 Source: www.bankrate.com as at July 2021.

40 Clark, 'Number of people employed in the United Kingdom'.

41 'What it's worth: Revisiting the value of financial advice', Royal London, no date, available at https://ilcuk.org.uk/wp-content/uploads/2019/11/ILC-What-its-worth-Revisiting-the-value-of-financial-advice.pdf (accessed 8 February 2022).

42 Helen Morrissey, 'We must tackle misconceptions fuelling advice gap as 9.4m people miss out – Royal London', Royal London, April 2021, available at www.royallondon.com/media/press-releases/press-releases-2021/april/we-must-tackle-misconceptions-fuelling-advice-gap-as-9.4m-people-miss-out--royal-london (accessed 12 November 2021).

43 These are shares in companies, and the term is widely used to mean shares in quoted companies that are traded on a major stock exchange.

44 'Financial advice provides £47,000 wealth uplift in a decade, new research from Royal London and ILC shows', ILC UK, 28 November 2019, https://ilcuk.org.uk/financial-advice-provides-47k-wealth-uplift-in-decade (accessed 12 November 2021).

45 Webb, 'Millions at risk with savings of £100 or less'.

46 'Exploring the advice gap', Royal London, April 2021, available at https://adviser.royallondon.com/globalassets/docs/adviser/misc/br4pd0007-exploring-the-advice-gap-research-report.pdf (accessed 8 February 2022).

47 In a letter dated 2 December 1887 to 'Mrs Foote', reprinted in the *Los Angeles Times* on 16 March 1930.

48 The Reading Agency, 'Reading facts', available at https://readingagency.org.uk/about/impact/002-reading-facts-1 (accessed 12 November 2021).

49 'Exploring the advice gap', Royal London.

50 'The accountancy profession in the UK', CCAB,
    November 2018, available at www.ccab.org.
    uk/wp-content/uploads/2020/06/The-
    Accountancy-Profession-in-the-UK-and-Ireland.
    pdf (accessed 8 February 2022).

Acknowledgements

In allowing me the time to focus on this book, I wish to thank the staff at Truly Independent Ltd for running the firm without me, and in particular Katie Brinsden who, like a swan, always looks unruffled but paddles like hell underneath; and Neil Jeffrey, who is rarely affected by anything and, in his own way, continues to develop relationships with existing and new advisers to the firm.

To all the advisers at Truly Independent, for your outstanding contribution to the growth of the firm and the professional way you engage with your clients. You do a great job.

To all at Rethink Press for their outstanding patience and support in encouraging me to complete the difficult second book.

Last but not least to Catherine, my wife, for giving me the time and space needed to think, contemplate and at times disappear into my own head. I do listen!

The Author

 Andrew Goodwin is the managing director and co-founder of national IFA Truly Independent Ltd and the author of *The Happy Financial Adviser* (Rethink Press, 2017).

His career in financial services started when he graduated from Heriot-Watt University in Edinburgh with an honours degree in Actuarial Mathematics and Statistics.

He worked for General Accident (now Aviva) as a senior financial consultant before moving into their corporate division where he achieved advanced qualifications in taxation and trusts, supervision and sales management, and pensions.

After joining national IFA Positive Solutions on a self-employed contract, he recruited and mentored others into a similar role. By 2008 he was head of the North division, in charge of his own team of business consultants.

Recognising that the industry was changing, Andrew left employment to set up his own multiadviser firm, Truly Independent Ltd in 2009. By 2020, Truly Independent Ltd had grown to an industry-recognised multi-million-pound firm of independent financial advisers distributed all across the UK. In 2021 Truly Independent launched an app called Vero, only available through their financial advisers. Andrew says, 'It's wealth in the palm of your hand!'

Andrew is constantly renovating and accumulating property and continually invests in tax-efficient equity plans. Always striving to be the best, he was a schools county chess player, a golf club champion and has a black belt in karate.

To learn more about Andrew go to:

⊕ www.trulyconnect.co.uk

in linkedin.com/in/andrew-goodwin

▢ https://twitter.com/TrulyIFA